A HISTORY OF SKATES IN CANADA

JEAN-MARIE LEDUC

WITH SEAN GRAHAM AND JULIE LÉGER

HERITAGE

Victoria | Vancouver | Calgary

Heritage House Publishing Company Ltd.
heritagehouse.ca

CATALOGUING INFORMATION AVAILABLE FROM
LIBRARY AND ARCHIVES CANADA
978-1-77203-227-7 (pbk)
978-1-77203-228-4 (epub)
978-1-77203-229-1 (epdf)

Edited by Lenore Hietkamp
Proofread by Kari Magnuson
Cover and interior design by Setareh Ashrafologhalai
Cover photographs (clockwise from top left): Maurice "The Rocket" Richard,
1957, LAC/National Film Board fonds/e011176705; Couple skating in Rotary Ice
Carnival, ca 1948, Jack Lindsay/City of Vancouver Archives; Orrin Markhus and
Irma Thomas, Ice Capades, Vancouver, 1962, Pacific National Exhibition/City of
Vancouver Archives, 180-6265; Figure skating, Ottawa, 1927, Dept. of Interior/
Library and Archives Canada/PA-043666; Young speedskaters, Calgary Alberta,
March 1973, *Calgary Herald*/Glenbow Museum/PA-1599-538-42; (centre photo)
"Hugger" hockey skates, Collection of Jean-Marie Leduc

Unless otherwise indicated, skates shown are from the collection of Jean-Marie
Leduc and photos were produced by René Lavoie.

The interior of this book was produced on FSC®-certified paper, processed
chlorine free and acid free.

We acknowledge the financial support of the Government of Canada through
the Canada Book Fund (CBF) and the Canada Council for the Arts, and the
Province of British Columbia through the British Columbia Arts Council
and the Book Publishing Tax Credit.

21 20 19 18 17   1 2 3 4 5
Printed in Canada

Contents

_____

*To my dear wife, Marie-Claire, who
for more than thirty-five years supported
me in the collecting of all these skates. Her
patience with this project has been end-
less, and for that, and so much more, I am
so grateful to have her by my side.*

_____

Preface

GROWING UP PLAYING hockey, I never gave much thought to my skates. I knew that I didn't like them too sharp and that new pairs were a pain to break in, but otherwise the skates were just another piece of equipment. Until a couple of years ago, I couldn't have explained how skates work, outside of saying that ice is slippery. Little did I know that I would have the unique opportunity to meet Jean-Marie Leduc and work with him on this book—after he explained the physics of skating, of course.

The idea for this book first came to my attention in the spring of 2014. I was preparing to defend my doctoral thesis at the University of Ottawa when my advisor, Dr. Damien-Claude Bélanger, mentioned that he had heard about Jean-Marie Leduc's collection and desire to write a book. Frankly, I didn't think much about it at the time, as the defence occupied the bulk of my attention, but a couple of months later, my good friend and colleague Julie Léger mentioned it. At that point, we were both working for the same historical research company and, while neither of us could commit all our time, we thought that this would be the perfect opportunity for a collaboration. So we talked about what a book on skates might look like and put together a pitch.

OPPOSITE "Skating Carnival," thought to be of the Victoria Skating Rink, Montreal, completed in 1862. Watercolour by Arthur Elliot, ca 1881. LAC, ACC. NO. R9266-220/PETER WINKWORTH COLLECTION OF CANADIANA

The first time we met Mr. Leduc was that summer and the three of us quickly got along. We each had our ideas for what the book should be, but we easily came to a consensus and got to work. While there were certainly obstacles, for the most part everyone found a role that was best for them. Mr. Leduc had the information, but we had to get it into a book. I genuinely enjoyed the next steps, regularly going to the Leducs' house to learn about skates. After hours of interviews, writing, and photographs, we had the informational basis of a book. It was all made easier by having Mrs. Leduc there every step of the way to keep an eye out and make sure we were staying on track—and her delicious soup didn't hurt either. Fortunately, Julie, who by that time had moved to Hamilton, had built our database and organized everything we had. From there, it was a matter of drafting the text, editing, and finding the right publisher.

What has been great about this project is how it has been successful despite the changing circumstances through which we worked. When we started, Julie was the mother of a beautiful baby girl and working full-time in Ottawa. Today, that daughter is in school and is a big sister, as Julie and her husband welcomed their second daughter this year. For my part, this project has followed me as I moved from Ottawa to work in Boston and then in China and back again. Through all the changes, the three of us have managed to work (somewhat) seamlessly, and we have produced a book that we really like.

SEAN GRAHAM

Ottawa, ON

Acknowledgements

FIRST WISH TO thank all those who gave me skates for my collection.

A special thank you goes to Dr. Sean Graham, who helped put this book together and spent three years collaborating with me to see this project to its conclusion. To Mrs. Julie Léger, who was instrumental in the coordination of our database and processing the piles of information required for this project; her contributions made this book possible. And to Nathalie Leduc, who never hesitated to help me with her computer when needed; she was essential in keeping everything on the right track.

I am extremely grateful to René Lavoie, our extremely talented photographer and my son-in-law. He rescued this project at the last minute and produced beautiful images of the skates in my collection. Those photos were also made possible by my daughter, Martine Leduc, who came to Ottawa to help with the laborious photo shoot. For the procurement of other images in this book, I wish to thank the Glenbow Museum, Library and Archives Canada, the Dartmouth Heritage Museum, the Dawson City Museum, the City of Vancouver Archives, the McCord Museum, the National Archives in the Netherlands, and Sylvain Leclerc from Montreal.

Many thanks to Lenore Hietkamp, Lara Kordic, and the entire team at Heritage House. They have been extremely supportive in this endeavour, helping me navigate the (sometimes) rocky terrain of publishing. This book is better because of their involvement.

I would also like to acknowledge everyone in the skating world whom I have had the pleasure of meeting over the years, from skaters to fans to coaches and officials. They say that it's not what you do but who you do it with that matters, and the skating community—across all the sports—has provided me with some great friends and cherished memories. Thank you!

And, of course, a huge thank-you my wife, who kept me on track with the proper skates.

JEAN-MARIE LEDUC
Ottawa, ON

A S THE SUN sets in Moncton, a group of kids on a frozen lake
furiously scramble to score the winning goal before darkness
sets in. In Ottawa, a grandfather holds his granddaughter's
hand as she steps onto the Rideau Canal to skate for the first time.
After a long training session, a speed skater leaves the arena at the
Olympic Oval in Calgary. In Jasper, a father floods his backyard
rink, while in White Rock, a figure skater celebrates after suc-
cessfully landing a triple Axel for the first time.

These vignettes from across the country are central to the
experience of Canadians. So many of us grew up on skates, learning to skate in the public arenas across the country, or on ponds
and lakes or in backyard rinks. People have keen memories of
family fun or personal achievements on the ice. Family nights
on skates and crack-the-whip. The save that preserved the lead
in a game of shinney. The perfect routine at the biggest competition of the year. Facing the full-sized oval for the first time.
Winning a race to the end of the river against all the kids in the
neighbourhood.

Through long winters with frigid winds and mountains of snow, Canadians take to the ice for fun, exercise, and competition. Every day, refusing to hibernate, millions of Canadians venture from the warmth of their homes to skate. Skating is so popular that even in summer Canadians flock to arenas to play hockey, speed skate, and figure skate. As a child, I walked three or four miles to watch the speed skating at Bingham Square and Anglesea Square in Ottawa. My parents did not like me going so far on my own, so I would sneak off without their knowing. I had to see the skaters. Their speed was amazing. I stood all day, mesmerized, watching them go round and round the rink. When I took up tennis, I appreciated skating even more: its individuality, the personal struggle to constantly improve. Seeing those elements in a winter sport forged my lifelong connection to skating.

The big game on skates that everyone at least knows about is hockey, Canada's national winter sport. Hockey's role in Canadian history has been explored in many books, and even Historica Canada has devoted several *Heritage Minutes* to it on television. Viewer ratings for games during the Olympics, NHL playoffs, or World Junior Championships are the highest for Canadian networks, and generations of Canadians grew up watching Maurice "Rocket" Richard, Gordie Howe, Paul Henderson, and Wayne Gretzky. Of course, it is not just hockey stars who capture the Canadian imagination. The figure skater Barbara Ann Scott was a national hero through much of the twentieth century and arguably the most popular Canadian athlete, winning an Olympic gold medal in figure skating in 1948, while skaters Gaétan Boucher, Catriona Le May Doan, and Charles Hamelin have been in the forefront of Canada's perennially strong speed skating teams.

Much has been written about Canadians' love affair with these sports, but it's the skate that makes it all possible. It is the metal under your foot that allows you to move on ice. From our

RIGHT Boy with a hockey stick and skates, Quebec City. 1955–1963. ROSEMARY GILLIAT EATON/LAC

earliest history, skates facilitated communication, transportation, and survival. They were used by First Nations to travel in winter. Settlers strapped them on for recreation, and sports competitors pushed designers to create skates with which they could leap higher, go faster, and be stronger.

People and their sports tell their own stories, and these stories have shaped the development of skates. The rules of figure skating have changed speed skating records are regularly broken, and hockey players perform more skilfully than fifty years ago because skate manufacturers produce better skates. This book tells the skate story.

THE LEDUC SKATE COLLECTION

I have always loved to watch skating. Because I have problems with my feet, though, I have never been able to skate. I passed along the one pair of skates I had to my cousin because I could not use them. Nevertheless, like Canadians all across the country, I fell in love with skating. In our Canadian culture of skating, athletes become cultural icons, enticing children to follow in their footstops. While not all children will become figure skating champions, they can take lessons to learn figure skating and eventually teach other children. Not all children will be selected for Junior Hockey teams, but they learn the game and many good skills along the way. And more and more children are learning to skate like speed skaters.

ABOVE "All Star" speed skates, designed by Bob Planert, Cambridge, Ontario, 1977. Jean-François Leduc (the author's son) wore these when he won a gold medal at the Canadian Speed Skating Championship in 1984. COLLECTION OF JEAN-MARIE LEDUC

When my son was five, I started taking him to the arena. Once his hockey-playing days ended—his coach said he was fast but too small for the sport—he started speed skating. From local races to provincial competitions and ultimately to national championships, he continued to improve, and he eventually won a Canadian title. Unfortunately, a knee injury ended his dreams prior to the 1992 Olympic games at Albertville.

I had discovered speed skating in my youth, and was thrilled that my son became a speed skater. My enthusiasm for the sport has never wavered; it is the winter sport with which I have the closest connection. Even though I do not skate, I have been deeply involved for over thirty years, serving as the president of the Ottawa Pacers Speed Skating Club and the Gloucester Concordes. I have spent much of my life as a race announcer. Speed skating announcers overlook the ice, and I introduced the skaters. During the race I described the event—essentially doing a play-by-play—for the spectators. I identified the finishing order, including race times. I also introduced medalists as they received their medals.

My first gig was at Winterlude in Ottawa in 1980, when the Pacers Speed Skating Club hosted the first North American skating marathon at Lac Beauchamp in Hull. The organizers asked me to be their bilingual announcer. After that, I became a regular announcer. From introducing athletes to keeping the crowd enthused to reporting the results, I relished my involvement in a sport I loved. I worked up the ranks, criss-crossing the country to announce at local, national, and international competitions. Once, I travelled to the Netherlands to announce an event. I felt it was a remarkable experience, given how the Dutch love speed skating—after all, it is their national sport. In Holland, I learned the proper way to call a race, which was invaluable to my career. The highlight for me was at the Olympic Games in Salt Lake City in 2002, when I announced in French for the central broadcasting system during the long-track speed skating competition.

While announcing at the Olympics was a once-in-a-lifetime experience, announcing skating competitions at the grassroots level has always been special. I liked keeping people excited and energized about the events on the ice, not always an easy task in longer races. Once I announced a race where a little girl competed for the first time. Her race was tough, as she kept falling down, but even after all the other skaters finished, she kept going. I kept the crowd interested and cheered her on to the end. When she reached the finish line, she saw everyone cheering. She looked up and asked, "Do I win a medal?"

During the 1980s, as president of the Ottawa Pacers Speed Skating Club, I organized the 1986 celebration of the centennial of Speed Skating Canada. Mulling over the best way to commemorate the event, it dawned on me to create a showcase of skates to highlight the sport's evolution. Little did I know where the idea would lead.

That showcase became the basis for my skate collection, which now includes over 350 pairs. My first pair came from Jack Barber, an Ottawa man who is now in the Speed Skating Canada Hall of Fame. He was a terrific skater and a wonderful man,

who once was mistakenly reported to have died in a car accident. When I told him I was looking for old skates, he gave me four pairs. I also acquired many from antique dealers, but as the collection grew and more people heard about it, I received calls from around the world about old iron skates found in a barn, family skates passed down through generations, and skates that elite athletes kept long after their retirement.

THE STORY OF A SKATE

Each pair tells a story, and whenever I get a new pair I try to figure out the story. Each skate presents an initial clue—a logo, a serial or patent number, or the material it's made from. The first step I take is to date the skates, which I usually accomplish by identifying the model. Most manufacturers only use a model for a certain time, which presents a date range. From there, patent numbers further narrow it down. Some models have multiple patent numbers because of small alterations to the skates, which is an accurate way to specify when a skate was made. After that, a closer examination of the skate often shows visual clues. Indicators of age and make include the type of metal, how a skate attaches to the foot, and the presence or absence of a boot. The length of the blade, the manner in which it is sharpened, and its general shape tells me what activity it was intended for, while its general condition indicates how it was cared for and how long it was used.

Sometimes I refer to collectors' guides and company records to confirm information. These identifiers are not always obvious from just looking at the skate. I also gather information from hockey, speed skating, and figure skating experts about the skates in each sport and how they differ. While some differences are obvious, others are subtle, and through consultation, I have acquired in-depth knowledge of my collection. Each pair undergoes this laborious process, a process I always find very satisfying.

My passion has led me to teach others about skates. My skates have appeared in exhibitions across the country, including at the Canadian Museum of History, the Hockey Hall of Fame, and the 2010 Olympic Winter Games in Vancouver. One of my favourite parts of these exhibitions is educating people about skates and how they have changed. Visitors are always interested to see how skates have evolved and how people used the early heavy, clunky designs. I love seeing people's reactions, particularly the emotional responses when they see skates like those they used in their youth. Both men and women are brought to tears when they find the skates they grew up with. Skates are reminders of hockey games with friends, Christmas with family, and dates with first loves. They are so much more than a piece of steel attached to a boot.

HOW SKATES WORK

The common conception of a skate includes the boot, but for most of skating history, skates did not include a boot. Rather than put your foot into a boot already connected to the skate, you attached the skate to your footwear with leather straps, screws, adjustable levers, or clamps. Boots are relatively new—within the last two hundred years—and thousands of people around the world still wear skates they attach to their shoes. As a result, the majority of the skates in my collection do not have boots, and for that reason, skates are really the part in contact with the ice. That includes

not only the blade but everything below the foot. All these things work together to glide over ice.

All skates work basically the same. The most common blade, the one we find on figure skates and hockey skates, is called a hollow ground blade. If you look at a blade from the front, the metal is usually just wide enough to have two edges on the inside and outside. These two edges are what actually come in contact with the ice, and they allow the skater to push into the ice with the inside or outside of the foot. Between the two edges, the metal is not flat but concave; when the blade is sharpened, it is the two edges that are actually affected. Some skates, like speed skates, are actually much thinner, without that hollow ground and without the two edges. As the blade moves over the ice, it creates a thin layer of water, reducing the friction between the ice and blade and allowing the skater to push forward. Without the thin layer of water, gliding would not be possible; it would be like moving on concrete. In fact, if you put oil on concrete, it functions the same as water on ice, reducing the friction and making it possible to skate. Resurfacing the ice—spreading a thin layer of water to freeze—makes it easier for the skate to move. An accumulation of snow on ice makes it more difficult to skate, as the snow inhibits the blade's ability to function.

Because the melting occurs where the blade touches the ice, the longer the blade, the more water is created. This explains why skates for long distances, like speed skates, have long blades: they generate more water, allowing the skaters to go faster and to expend less effort in skating a great distance. One year during Winterlude in Ottawa, the Capital Long Blade Skating Club held an exhibition on the Rideau Canal where we pitted a skater against a horse. Our skater, Michel van Musschenbroek, only had three weeks to train, but still accepted the challenge. On a beautiful Sunday afternoon, in front of fifty thousand spectators, Michel raced a horse. Because of the way the reins sat on the horse, the horse had to be moving to breathe and to start running. Michel waited at the start line while the horse trotted toward him. When the horse reached the start line, the gun was fired and they were off. As the horse was already warmed up, it raced out to an early advantage, but with his long blades Michel made up the difference and won the race by twenty-five feet. It was one of the fastest performances I ever witnessed from a skater. It was a terrific example of the speed achieved using long blades. Today, elite skaters reach sixty-one kilometres per hour.

THE RIGHT SKATES

There are different kinds of skates because for each activity there is the "right" skate. Many people learn to skate as children, and they learn on the short blades of hockey or figure skates, nudging the new skater in the direction of figure skating or playing hockey. The short blades of hockey and figure skates allow the quick turns, stops, and manoeuvres of the sports. And so many adult Canadians use short blades for recreational skating, even though long blades are actually better suited to a leisurely glide around a rink or down a canal.

Since metal skates were invented over five hundred years ago, what constituted the right skates has drastically changed. This book traces the evolution of how they evolved and improved, contributing to the development of sports that are popular around the world. From the skates used in the Mesolithic period to those used by the fastest speed skaters today, this book charts their development. The earliest skates were made of bone, then came the first wood skates, followed by metal skates, without and later with boots. Metal skates allowed for greater specialization, and different sports grew popular as a result. Skates designed for speed, skates for playing hockey, and figure skates all evolved differently, meeting the needs of different athletes. My collection also features skates that do not fit these categories, whether they be skates worn by world-class athletes, skates used for decorative purposes, or skates whose designs were not "up to snuff."

Whenever I exhibit my skate collection, visitors ask if any were worn by well-known athletes. They are hoping for Gordie Howe or Wayne Gretzky, Hayley Wickenheiser, Cindy Klassen, or Kurt Browning. When I say no, people are surprised—they expect the skates of at least a few famous athletes to be featured in such a large collection. But my interest is the story of skates, and the fact that a famous athlete owned a certain pair does not necessarily contribute to that story, so I have not sought out the skates of famous athletes. Those skates are certainly good memorabilia, but memorabilia does not characterize the skates in the collection. However, whenever my skates are included in an exhibition, people always want to see "personality skates," so I have pairs from Barbara Ann Scott, "Joe" Lépine, "Butch" Bouchard, and Gaétan

ABOVE Skating on the
St. Lawrence, Montreal,
Quebec, 1896. LAC, ACC.
NO. 1970-188-1668/W.H.
COVERDALE COLLECTION
OF CANADIANA

Boucher. I have included those in this book because they illustrate skates of a certain make and model; that they were worn by a notable athlete only adds to their interest.

In addition to the personality skates, certain pairs do not really fit any category. Some were experiments, others were custom made, and a couple were failed designs. They do not represent a major change in skates and skate design, but they are important because they were part of the process. The experiments led to improvements, personalized pairs help explain the specialization in these sports, and the failures demonstrate the process of skate design. Some look strange, others seem funny, but they all tell a story and are part of skating's history.

For thousands of years, skates have been used by people to survive, travel, exercise, and compete. Skates are a vital piece of Canada's story, and their development is entangled with our own process of growing up, and yet we know little about their history. Everyone, even someone who has never skated, like myself, has some connection to skating. It's a national pastime! Yet the skates themselves, the things that make those special memories possible, are often overlooked. This is their story.

Skates for Beginners

LEARNING HOW TO skate is a rite of passage for many Canadians. Losing your balance, slipping, falling, blisters: certain designs can help beginners avoid these problems.

I have always maintained that if you want to learn how to skate, pick up a pair of long blades, even if they are the sort you have to strap onto your boots. They are so much easier to begin on than short blades. Falling down on long blades is not easy to do—not only are they longer but they have a smaller rocker, which makes balance much easier to maintain. On hockey or figure skates, you can fall to the side or forward or backward. On long skates, you can only fall to the side. And if you start with long blades, moving to short blades is easy. My wife tried long blades for the first time at the age of forty-eight. She trained for two hours a week over six weeks before signing up for

ABOVE Children wearing training skates, on their neighbourhood skating rink, corner of 5th Ave. and 11 ½ St. NW, Calgary, Alberta, ca 1920. GLENBOW MUSEUM, NA-5336-23

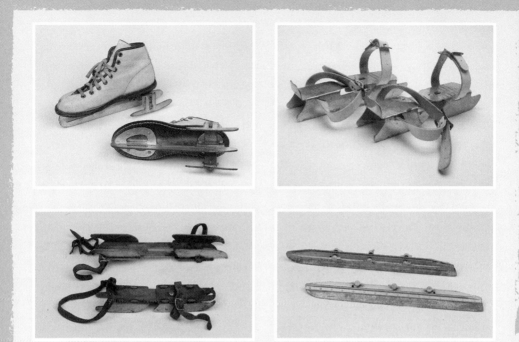

TOP, LEFT "Tri-blade" training skate, Sault Ste Marie, ON, 1940. COLLECTION OF JEAN-MARIE LEDUC

TOP, RIGHT Cheese cutters, 20th century. M2004.65.3.1-2 © MCCORD MUSEUM

BOTTOM, LEFT "Bob" skate by Samuel Winslow Skate Manufacturing Co., Worcester, MA, 1901. COLLECTION OF JEAN-MARIE LEDUC

BOTTOM, RIGHT "Finlam" blade, Finland, 1980S. COLLECTION OF JEAN-MARIE LEDUC

a one-hundred-kilometre marathon on the Rideau Canal. She won the medal for the longest distance travelled by a woman in that race. Even with such little time on the ice before the race, she never fell and was able to skate more than ten lengths of the canal—eighty-six kilometres.

This message has not spread far, though, particularly not in Canada, where short blades for hockey are the norm, and where girls seem

to still use figure skates, which are only slightly longer than hockey skates and are quite heavy. But because it can be so difficult to learn on short blades, people have designed other skates that make it easier for beginners and children when they first strap a pair to their feet.

One of the most popular strategies was to incorporate the same principle as training wheels on bikes: add additional blades. One pair in the collection, made in 1940, has two small blades bolted to the heel to help skaters keep their balance, and is an example of the "tri-blade" training skates of the period. The extra blades are not there to be skated on—they have no edges—but, like training wheels on a bike, are there to ensure that the skater does not fall. As the skater gets more comfortable on the skates, the outside blades can be raised in stages so that they are less likely to touch the ice, and eventually they can be removed completely, or the skater graduates to a new pair.

More popular for training than the tri-blade, however, was the "cheese cutter," which is still in use today. The cheese cutter, which resembles the kitchen device, is even easier to use than the tri-blade because it has four blades. A beginner could not actually skate with cheese cutters—it is nearly impossible to push back and out on those blades—but they let people get a feel for the ice. Instead of skating, a person wearing cheese cutters would be able to walk and maybe glide a little on the ice without having to balance on a single blade. It lets a beginner get a feel for what it is like to stand on ice with blades, serving as an entry to skating.

A similar concept but different design comes in the form of the "Bob" skate. Produced by the Samuel Winslow Manufacturing Company in Worcester, Massachusetts, in 1901, these skates resemble a bobsleigh, hence the name. They are strapped to the foot at the toe and heel and are quite versatile because they can be lengthened or shortened through the middle, depending on the size of the skater's foot. A wing nut under the toe can be loosened, allowing the front to be adjusted as needed. This is probably not the most effective means of teaching someone to skate, but they were popular and thousands of people hit the ice for the first time with these on their feet.

About thirty years ago, some designers in Finland came up with an idea that would allow kids to break in their new hockey skates while still learning on a long blade. Made through the 1980s, this design, called "Finlam," has a slot through the top of the blade that would fit a hockey or figure skate blade. The goal was to initiate and promote the use of long blades in recreational skating, racing, and marathon skating in Finland. The hope was that people would use these with their hockey and figure skates, realize how much easier it is to skate with long blades, and eventually switch. Given how reluctant Canadians seem to be about buying long blades, I think these would be a good compromise to help teach kids how to skate. Once they have it mastered, they could take these off and start crashing the net or landing the triple Axel. Even though the tri-blade and the cheese cutter were intended to serve as training skates, these would be much more effective.

Early
Skates

SKATES AND CULTURE

ABOVE Happy New Year card from Quebec, between 1873 and 1878. Greeting card, G. & W. Clarke's second Scenic Series. LAC, ARCH. REF. NO. R11648, ALBUM 9, ITEM 22

A THIRTEEN-YEAR-OLD girl gleefully skates on a frozen pond with a group of friends in the Dutch town of Schiedam. All of sudden she loses her balance and falls to the ice. When her friends rush over to attend to her, it is clear the injuries are severe: three broken ribs and a broken hip. After returning to her bed, she is in constant pain and cannot walk. The girl remains bedridden for the rest of her life.

This tragic accident happened in 1403 and the unfortunate girl, who for decades suffered from her skating injuries before her death in 1433, was Lidwina. Despite the pain, she never complained and maintained a strong faith in God. As she passed her days in bed, she prayed constantly, not for her own recovery, but for others. Despite her own hardships, she prayed for those who were less fortunate and who, in her mind, were more deserving of God's help. That devotion was inspiring and, with miracles reported at her bedside, she became a revered figure

in the Catholic Church for her unwavering devotion and spirit. Following her death, her grave became a site of pilgrimage for Catholics throughout Europe, and in 1434 a chapel was built over her final resting place—if you visit Schiedam today, you can visit the Basilica of Lidwina, which was completed in 1905. Over 400 years after Lidwina's death, on March 14, 1890, she was canonized by Pope Leo XIII.

Lidwina is now the patron saint of skating. That skating warrants a patron saint certainly speaks to its popularity around the world. In the twenty-first century that popularity is largely due to skating as a sport, but skating was first a means of survival for millions of people. And it is not just the Catholics who have a religious figure tied to skating. The Norse god Ullr has been described as a wizard with a cunning way of travelling across snow and ice. In modern depictions he typically wears skates or skis—he was reputed to be a master of both—and is the god of snow and skiing. The earliest Norse skaters also revered Skadi, the Norse goddess of winter and the hunt.

The connection between religion and skating may not seem clear today, but at its earliest, skating was a lifeline for people. Otherwise unable to traverse ice and snow, skates and skating allowed people to hunt, find shelter, and communicate through long winters. Being so essential to survival, it is easy to see how people turned to religion to both declare their thanks for their skates and to pray for their safety while skating. While not a matter of life and death today, people still turn to religion in matters of skating—although now it is mostly to pray for a big save when the home team is short-handed.

Skating has been around for millennia. According to John Misha Petkevich, in *The Skater's Handbook*, the first literary reference to skates appears in *Elder Edda*, a collection of Norse mythical and heroic poems. The book was transcribed in the thirteenth century, but most of the poems are from the tenth century or earlier. The poems largely discuss the practical reasons why someone would have skated through the Middle

Ages, but they also highlight how vital skating was throughout Nordic history.

North America does not have the same literary history as Europe, so textual references to skates appear only after European colonization. Even though we may not have a written source, we know that Canada's Indigenous peoples made skates long before contact with Europeans. Stories about skating have been passed down among Indigenous people. Early skating artifacts also exist, and explorers from Europe, such as Samuel de Champlain and Pierre Dugua, Sieur de Mons, wrote about seeing Indigenous people using skates.

BONE SKATES

The earliest skates in North America were made of bone. Indigenous craftsmen made the buffalo bone pair in my collection between ten thousand and fifteen thousand years ago, somewhere in what is now Canada. The craftsmen selected a relatively flat bone, ensuring it would be easy to place on the foot. Holes were drilled into the ends of the bone for the leather straps used to tie the skate to the foot. This type of skate does not resemble a modern skate, so the most common question I get is, "How did people skate on that?"

It is a good question, as the wide base creates quite a bit of friction against the ice, and the lack of an edge makes it all but impossible to use a typical skating motion. What is important to remember, however, is that the skating movement on these bones was completely different than skating today. Where today skaters extend their legs backwards to push themselves forward, these skates required the use of a pole. Skaters would stand straight up and use the pole to propel themselves across the ice. So rather than use the edge of the skate to power their movements, skaters on bones used their arms to provide the forward momentum.

TOP Buffalo bone skates, 10,000 to 15,000 years old. COLLECTION OF JEAN-MARIE LEDUC

MIDDLE Whale bone skates, appr. 2,900 years old. COLLECTION OF JEAN-MARIE LEDUC

BOTTOM Buffalo rib skates, Wyoming area, appr. 2,000 years old. COLLECTION OF JEAN-MARIE LEDUC

The bone provided a surface that could glide over ice easily, creating a faster way to traverse a frozen lake or river than using regular footwear.

Like all skates, those made from bone continued to evolve over time. The major change was in the width. The wider the bone, the more contact it made with the ice; this increase of friction slows down the skater. Indigenous peoples used buffalo rib bones for their skates, as well as the front leg bones from deer and reindeer. The middle pair on the previous page, made of whale bone about 2,900 years ago, shows how craftsmen experimented with different materials and designs for skates. From the side, the shape slightly resembles a modern skate; they are much thinner compared to the previous pair. The pair from what is now Wyoming also required a pole for forward propulsion, and because they are thinner, they moved forward easier, although the skater had to work harder to maintain balance. A new skater might have started on the wider pair then graduated to the rib bone, once they mastered the technique of skating on bones.

One of the questions I have been asked about bone skates is if you are using a pole to push yourself forward, how is it different from skiing? To me, the biggest difference is the surface on which you move. The bones in my collection were used primarily on ice, so that makes them skates. First Nation peoples had different implements for moving across the snow, and bones were reserved for the ice, thus making them skates. Of course, there is a close relationship between bone skates and skiing, and that distinction is not always clear. In fact, as Lynn Copley-Graves explains in *Figure Skating History: The Evolution of Dance on Ice*, Norwegians called both skating and skiing *ondur*.

Not surprisingly, bone skates are the most difficult to preserve. I keep them separate from the rest of the collection and wrap them in more protective material than any other pair. Even with all those precautions, accidents can still happen. At an exhibition a few years ago, a little boy was holding one of my bone skates—a skate that was 2,900 years old—and it slipped out of his hand. The end broke into four or five pieces. The pieces were more like fragments that had come off the end of the bone. I was able to glue most of them back together. Handling material that is thousands of years old needs to be done very carefully.

Discovering the story of a pair of bone skates requires a different kind of sleuthing than understanding the story of a modern pair. Bone skates have no patent numbers, no metal components, and no model name to help identify them. There is also very little written about bone skates other than acknowledging that before metal skates, people in cold climates around the world attached bones to their feet to get around in the winter. The shape of bone skates is a good clue that they are intended as skates, and the holes for the leather straps are another indicator for how the bones were used. Figuring out when they were made is more difficult, so I have taken them to be appraised and dated by scientific experts who have been able to place approximate ages on each pair. The dates may not be exact, but they do give a good indication about skating at a specific time prior to the invention of metal skates.

METAL BLADES

Pieces of wood attached to the feet were likely in use too, possibly as early as the bone skates, but the only evidence is from ancient Norse stories. Likely by the thirteenth century, people in the Netherlands began to move on ice by strapping on wood blocks to which were attached long pieces of iron, and pushed themselves along with poles. Metal blades, like those we are familiar with, which are thin enough to have edges on either side of the blade that can be skated on, seem to have first appeared in the fifteenth

century, although there is some debate as to who made the first pair and where. It is generally accepted that it was in either the Netherlands or Norway, and at some point between 1452 and 1562. The distinction between the years is the difference between a metal blade inserted into wood stock, which I tend to call a wood skate, and a metal skate whose blade is incorporated into a metal footplate. While that debate continues, what is clear is that metal blades were used in the fifteenth century.

OPPOSITE Making skates. From the NFB photo story "Keep Country on Ice," 1956. PHOTO BY CHRIS LUND. LAC/NATIONAL FILM BOARD FONDS/ E011176410

The blade, of iron or steel, was a piece of metal with very different properties from a blade of bone or wood. It was strong enough to be thin, with edges that could dig into the ice, for forward propulsion, but just wide enough that the friction created by the blade on ice during forward movement would melt that important thin layer of water between the ice and the metal, smoothing the way for faster propulsion, eliminating any need for poles. Skaters then developed a technique similar to the one skaters use today. By extending the leg backwards and using the edge of the blade to propel the body forward, fifteenth-century skaters were developing a form of skating that not only was more efficient than using bones or wood platforms with iron runners, propelled with poles, but has also stood the test of time. As metal blades became more common, skaters adapted their style to fit with the new technology. In fact, as Copley-Graves explains, Dutch skaters began to be divided into two groups: those who preferred to skate on the inside edge of their skates and those who preferred the outside edge.

The edges are vital to skates—if you buy a new pair of skates and do not put an edge on the blades, you'll have a tough time standing up, let alone skating. Today, different edges are created for different sports, but Canadians usually sharpen their skates so that the bottom of the blade is shaped into a slight concave. The concave shape has two edges that touch the ice, so a skater can start or stop with either side of the foot, which is important in sports like hockey and figure skating. Since speed skaters do not need that same versatility, they use different edges on their skates, which we will see later.

Also vital to skating on metal blades is the direct contact with ice—they are not for use on both snow and ice. Anyone who has ever had to walk through a snow bank to retrieve a wayward puck or tried to play shinny in a snowstorm knows how hard snow can be on metal blades. Snow, even when it is as tightly packed as a (potentially) painful snowball, does not provide a hard enough surface. That is why, during an NHL game, people come out with shovels several times throughout the game to clear ice shavings from the ice.

EUROPEAN DESIGN
OF METAL AND WOOD

Of course, you cannot just strap a blade to your foot; not only would you not be able to stand, but you would probably hurt yourself. You need something between the blade and your foot: a footplate. Before the invention of all-metal skates, the footplate was a piece of wood. The type of wood depended on the location, but hardwood stands up to the wear and tear of skates. The Dutch skates in my collection, mass-produced by the Staal Company, are based on a Norwegian model that follows a model first produced in 1452 by a company called C & Co., which is visible on the blade. I acquired this pair from Speed Skating Canada in the 1980s for $35. The acorn adorning the toe of each skate is a trademark of the Staal Company. Leather straps connected the skate to the foot. By placing the blade into a slot underneath the footplate, these skates were not only more versatile than bones, but they were also strong enough to withstand the pressure applied by the skater in motion.

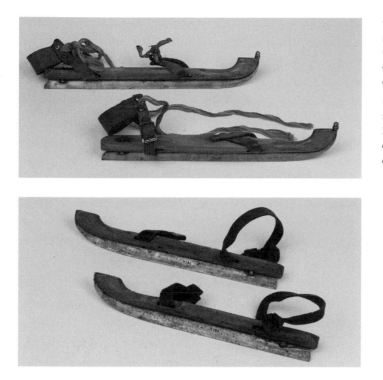

TOP Skates with blade set in wood stock, Staal Company, Dutch, 15th century. COLLECTION OF JEAN-MARIE LEDUC

BOTTOM Pleasure skate, manufactured in IJlst, Friesland (Netherlands), ca 1450. COLLECTION OF JEAN-MARIE LEDUC

The Dutch developed a similar skate. A pair from the 1450s, one of the oldest skates in my collection, is similar to the Norwegian model, with leather straps and a blade inserted into a slot in the wood beneath the foot. The skate extends well beyond the skater's toes, while the back of the skate lines up with the heel. This makes it a little harder to maintain balance if a skater happens to lean back, but the priority in the design was to make forward movement easy, to travel down the long canals of the Netherlands. And by extending the blades so far in front of the toes, it is nearly impossible to fall forward when wearing these skates.

These skates were an important part of military campaigns, at least in the Netherlands. During the Dutch revolt against the

Spanish in the sixteenth century, in the reign of the Duke of Alva, as James R. Hines relates in *Figure Skating: A History*, the Dutch fleet found itself trapped in the ice around Amsterdam. They cut a moat around their ships, thwarting the Spanish forces who arrived on foot. Retreating down the ice, the Spanish were surprised by Dutch musketeers on skates, whose mobility helped win that battle. Alva responded by ordering 7,000 pairs of skates, but no other battle on ice has been recorded. Fortunately, today wood skates have fallen out of favour with armed forces and are reserved for recreational purposes in some countries.

While these skates may look old-fashioned, such skates continue to be used. Many people find that wood platforms absorb the impact of skating better than other material, especially metal, and so they have persisted into the twenty-first century alongside the development of the all-metal skate. A company in the Netherlands still makes skates with a wood base—25,000 pairs a year—and they are so popular that you have to get your order in very early if you want them in time for the skating season.

Ice and Snow

ITH RIVER OR snow skates, a skater can cross a snow-covered lake or river, a necessity when travelling on natural ice in the winter. When skating with a normal pair of skates, a snowdrift can stop a skater in their tracks. People added skis to their skates to get around. In Canada, many of these were made in Montreal and on the East Coast, where people have long been using frozen bodies of water as paths to somewhere. Of course, people in the West also had to do this, but by the time settlers began to populate Western Canada in great numbers, they could simply order skates from the East Coast, which was already known for its quality river skates. Before this, Indigenous peoples used bone skates to cross rivers and lakes, occasionally switching to snowshoes as the conditions warranted, a strategy that the earliest settlers and fur traders in Western Canada also adopted.

For the most part, the popularity of river skates peaked in the early 1870s, when rivers and lakes used for transportation began to be cleared of snow regularly, but that does not mean they stopped being made. A great pair from the 1880s, a model known as the "Buddy Snow Skate," was made in upstate New York. The sticker featuring the model name is still visible on the front curl. A one-inch-wide sheet of

TOP "Buddy Snow Skate," made in New York, ca 1880. COLLECTION OF JEAN-MARIE LEDUC

MIDDLE Snow skate by Enfield Knoll Inc., 1896. COLLECTION OF JEAN-MARIE LEDUC

BOTTOM Long-distance skates, Swedish, 1980s. COLLECTION OF JEAN-MARIE LEDUC formed steel runs along the base, connected to the wood footplate by nails at the heel and toes, and provides the surface on which the wearer would be able move on the ice. Using these skates would require a similar technique to using bone skates, most effective on snow that had been tightly packed by a horse-drawn sleigh or hardened from a little rain. A similar design, made by Enfield Knoll Inc. in 1896, also features a wood platform for the foot, along with the leather strap to attach the skate to the foot.

Early skates had a strong connection to skiing, because of the need to travel over both ice and snow, and the Swedish have taken that to a whole new level. A pair made in the 1980s, with a reinforced steel blade and aluminum footplate, came into my collection via the Swedish Embassy in Ottawa. The blade is extremely thin, as it is intended to be used outdoors and on long stretches. The key to the design, however, is that ski boots can be clipped into the skate. So if you are already a skier, you do not need to break in new boots or mess around with leather straps or claps to step from the snow to the ice. The length can be adjusted by about three inches to account for different foot sizes. Because not all ski boots are the same, there are four different models to fit with the various boot fittings. These skates are quite versatile, popular with people who like to camp or do other outdoor activities in the winter. If you are on a frozen river and do not have river skates, for instance, something like this can be quite helpful. You can strap your skis and poles to your back and, when you hit snow, just switch out the blades for the skis without having to take off your boots. In Sweden, where the skates were made, these activities are so popular that laws were created to ensure everyone's safety. It is illegal to skate alone on rivers and lakes. You must also take safety equipment with you, including an inflatable bag around your neck and ski poles with a female and male tread so that poles from different sets can be screwed together to help pull someone out of the water.

Skates that you attach to footwear are still in use today, though not so much in Canada as in Europe. The main benefit of any skate with a platform is that you get to wear your own boots or shoes when skating, avoiding the painful blisters caused by new boots. By connecting the boot to the front of the footplate, in the same way that a boot connects to a ski, the skate essentially turns into a clap skate. This allows the skater's heel to start forward with the blade staying on the ice a little longer. The longer the skate is in contact with the ice, the faster and more efficient the skater can be. In addition, most blades on these bootless skates are longer than hockey or figure skates. The extended blade is easier to skate on (see "Skates for Beginners" on page 18), plus they are less expensive and require no more maintenance than other skates. Finally, for anyone who skates on rivers or canals, such as marathon skaters, where fewer turns are required than on a regular ice rink, these long skates are better than hockey or figure skates. They are not the best for speed or agility, but they are great for getting out on the ice for exercise and for going mostly in a straight line down a river or canal.

While the popularity of skates with wood platforms declined in the nineteenth century, they continued to be made. One model is the pair made in Canada in 1840 from blacksmith files, which naturally produces the two edges on either side of the blade that are typical of the skates we are familiar with today. The curl at the toe is the handle of the file. The wood stock is handcrafted from maple, a sturdy base for the skater. Another pair made ten years later has a similar style and the platform is also maple. Like other wood skates of this time, they were primarily used for recreational skating. The main difference between the two pairs is the length of the curl at the front of the skate, but they represent the main style of wood skates around the middle of the nineteenth century.

TOP Skates hand-crafted by a blacksmith, Canadian, ca 1840. COLLECTION OF JEAN-MARIE LEDUC

BOTTOM Skates hand-crafted using maple wood, English, ca 1850. COLLECTION OF JEAN-MARIE LEDUC

Works of Art

SOMETIMES SKATES CAN be actual works of art. One pair, a traditional Dutch wood skate that attached to the foot with straps or screws, is based upon an old model of Dutch skates that is still used today (the type that can be seen in Dutch art dating to 1498), and the skates were handpainted in the twentieth century to protect the wood. The scenes on each skate are slightly different—one shows a house while the other features a windmill—and both depict a skater on a river set against a beautiful mountainous background. The runners are stamped with "G. Ruiter G.S. Ruiter Bolsward" (Netherlands), the original manufacturers of the skates.

Lest you think that these are purely decorative pieces, they have seen plenty of ice time. These skates came from the postmaster of Giethoorn, Netherlands, whose great-grandfather had purchased them before beginning a tradition of passing them to the next generation. The postmaster never had children, though, so she decided to have them painted to protect the wood and then used them as a wall ornament.

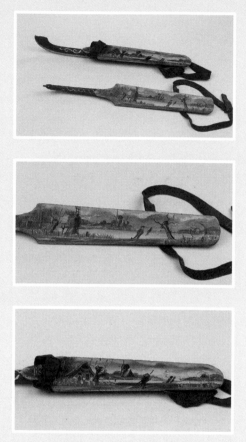

ABOVE Handpainted skates, Netherlands, based on model dating to 1498. COLLECTION OF JEAN-MARIE LEDUC

Starr "Acme"
(Trade Mark Registered)

THIS is the original self-fastening steel skate so famous throughout the world. It is perfect in adjustment. Sole clamps are independently adjustable. Skate can be placed centrally on the boot or on either side of a central line, thus accommodating any peculiarity in the shape of the foot. This is an exclusive feature in the Starr "Acme Club." Beware of German and other imitations. Be sure the name "Acme Club" and "Starr Mfg. Co." are on the runner. Sizes: 7 to 12½ inches.

Catalogue No. 100. Solid Steel, Unplated.   Price per pair, $1.75
Catalogue No. 101. Solid Steel, Nickel Plated.   Price per pair, $2.25

MORE INNOVATIONS

While plenty of people continued to use the skates I've described so far, they began to give way to others that would allow greater speed. Stronger and often lighter materials and different designs contributed to skates that could glide faster and handle the increased pressures. And so all-metal skates found their way to rinks. Rather than use straps to attach the skate to the foot, manufacturers developed clamps to ensure that the skate would be a snug fit. The first skates to used such clamps were developed by the Starr Manufacturing Company in the 1820s. Based in Halifax, Starr's sterling reputation and quality skates made them a leader in the industry in the nineteenth century. Just like skates with wood footplates, all-metal skates would attach to the skater's feet, but with the clamp, the foot had less chance of slipping.

The Starr Manufacturing Company gets plenty of credit for introducing clamps to their skates, but they were actually using the design of a man who never made a pair of skates himself: E.V. Bushnell. In 1848 Bushnell designed the first spring skate, which, by using a spring in the clamp, would have an even tighter connection to the foot and was much more comfortable because

ABOVE "Acme" skates, Starr Manufacturing Company, Dartmouth, Nova Scotia. COURTESY DARTMOUTH HERITAGE MUSEUM

you did not have straps wrapped around your feet and ankles. In his *Figure Skating: A History*, Hines says that this was a tremendous improvement because it made a rigid skate that was easy to put on. Bushnell sold his design for $25 to John Forbes, who produced 25 million pairs for the Acme Skate Company, selling them anywhere from 75¢ to $2.50, depending on the model and the materials used.

One of those pairs that is based on Bushnell's design is by Forbes, dating to 1883. They are recreational skates that feature a mechanical device at the toe to adjust the clamps. At the heel, a lever activates a cam to help secure the heel of the boot. At that point the lever is locked at the top of the runner. Patented in October 1883, the Forbes "New Skates," as he called them, were a major step forward in skate design. But Forbes could not sustain the business—his prices were too low—and eventually he had to declare bankruptcy, leaving the design to the Starr Manufacturing Company.

Certainly, Bushnell and Forbes were not the only ones who contributed to the improved design of skates. Henry Boswell, a member of the original Oxford Skating Club, which formed in Oxford, England, in 1838, liked to experiment with skate length. According to Copley-Graves, Boswell came up with the idea of removing part of the toe, extending the heel, for support, and then shaping the toe and heel into a curve. This helped with balance, which improved the accuracy of skaters in the club and is why his designs were often referred to as club skates.

The improvements are seen in a series of designs from the middle of the century. One of Bushnell's designs, reminiscent of older skates, has big leather straps attached to a wood footplate. Produced by Acme, the blade is stamped with the words "Genuine Acme Club Skate." While the year of production is not known, it would have been during Acme's run, which lasted from 1848 until

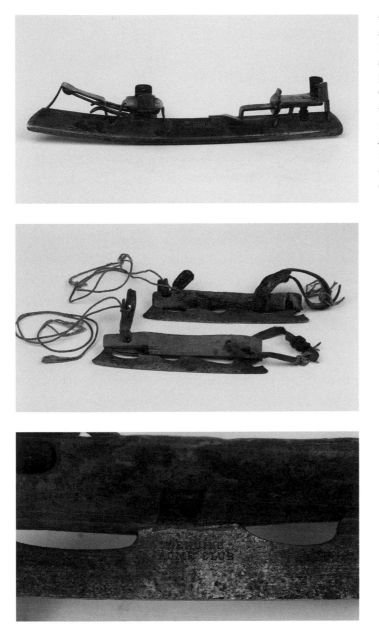

1865. You can also see how one of the skates has been repaired and also shows the original red paint on the wood base.

ALL-METAL EXPERIMENTS

In a pair from just a few years later, the club skate has lost its leather straps and wood base. In their place is a metal footplate and clamps on the sides of the skate. The clamps activate a cam, which secures the toes and heel while simultaneously locking on the blade under the heel for increased stability. The patent stamp on the blade indicates that they were made by the Starr Manufacturing Company in Halifax at some point after 1874.

Each pair made by Starr around this time has multiple patent stamps on the blade. A stamp indicating a patent date of 1875 tells us that not only were they produced a year later but they also contain differences, even minor ones, from the slightly older skates. The need to patent each change in the skates was important because in a competitive marketplace, companies were constantly looking to capitalize on what was popular with skaters. As a result, designs were heavily protected, and it is common for skates to have elements from multiple patents.

Those fears were not without merit, as the added strength and stability made clamp skates extremely popular, and other manufacturers began to get on board. The Keene Manufacturing Company in Torrington, Connecticut, produced a skate between 1854 and 1888, made from cast steel, which clamped to the skater's foot at the heel and toe and was adjusted with a key. You would just step into them wearing your own boots or shoes and the clamps would tighten around your foot. In addition to the added stability, the shorter blade made it possible to be more agile on the ice. This was important for the development of the modern form of hockey (different from the more informal game of shinny), as we'll see later.

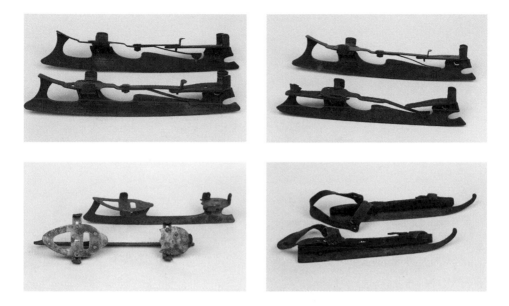

The introduction of all-metal skates not only expanded the market for skates, but it also brought into the industry a new group of skate manufacturers: blacksmiths. Even before skates were made of all metal, blacksmiths are known to have participated in the production process. They would make the blades, then send the blade on to a woodworker to add the footplate. The work of a blacksmith is evident in the blade of a rare pair made around 1760. The teeth and notches indicate that the blade is a pair of rasps. The footplate contains three openings for straps to secure the skate to the foot. The pair of blades in my collection made in the 1830s by a blacksmith are ready to be shipped to a woodworker. The wood footplate would be inserted under the hook toward the front and rest on the flat area at the back, to help stabilize the foot.

Only a blacksmith who was also a woodworker could produce the entire skate. To find a complete product from a blacksmith's shop, therefore, is unusual. The pair made by a blacksmith in

TOP, LEFT "No. 5 Acme Club Forbes'" skates, produced in Halifax, NS, after 1874. COLLECTION OF JEAN-MARIE LEDUC

BOTTOM, LEFT Cast steel skates by Keene Manufacturing Co., Torrington, CT, late 19th century. COLLECTION OF JEAN-MARIE LEDUC

TOP, RIGHT "Acme Club Skates" produced by Starr Manufacturing Co., Halifax, NS, 1875. COLLECTION OF JEAN-MARIE LEDUC

BOTTOM, RIGHT Pleasure skates, hand-made by a blacksmith, Dutch, mid-18th century. COLLECTION OF JEAN-MARIE LEDUC

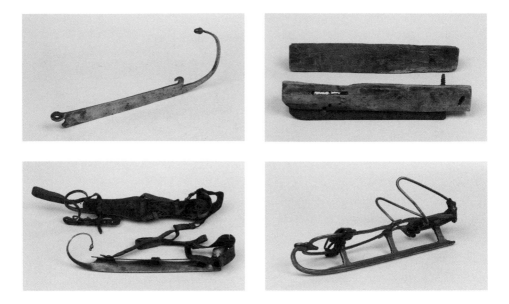

Merrickville, Ontario, during the construction of the Rideau Canal, sometime between 1826 and 1830, would attach to the foot with leather straps threaded through the base. The footplate is a bit thinner than some skates, so they were probably not very comfortable to skate on, but they are a good example of how black-smiths have long been involved in the manufacturing of skates.

With the increased popularity of all-metal skates, blacksmiths could not only produce the whole skate, but they could also hand-craft their own models. And there is something to be said for blacksmith skates. They are usually made from one piece of metal, making them stronger than all-metal skates made of separate parts. Generally crafted from iron or unfinished steel, they can be identified by their unique black colour, the result of being torched during production. They can also be customized so that they fit perfectly on a customer's footwear, thus reducing the possibility of slipping. On the other hand, because blacksmiths tended to use iron or unfinished steel, which was less expensive than stainless or polished steel, their skates were thicker and heavier than other all-metal skates. The customization also made them more expensive. Beginning around the middle of the nineteenth century, as the demand for all-metal skates rose dramatically, blacksmiths around the world started making some of the best skates ever seen.

One particular pair made by a blacksmith is fascinating not only for its uniqueness, but also because the blacksmith's great-granddaughter contributed them to my skate collection. Made in 1823, in St. Croix, Nova Scotia, these steel skates came with an O-ring, for carrying the skates and for hanging the skates to dry. With leather straps to attach the skate to the foot, they are similar to skates of that time that had wood footplates. However, the leather is bolted to the footplate to ensure a tight fit, while the raised piece at the heel also helps to ensure the foot is secure in the skate. Where other all-metal skates were moving toward clamps rather than straps, leather remained common for blacksmiths. This is not surprising—blacksmiths used one piece of metal to make skates so it would be difficult to also have the moving parts necessary for a clamp design. As we've seen, some partnered with woodworkers, but the majority preferred leather in their skates.

There was, however, no universal way in which the leather connected the skate to the foot. For instance, one style was to add metal slots to the sides of the base for the straps, a trademark of the Robert Gibson Co. in Birmingham, Connecticut, which patented the design in 1865. The pair in my collection is a copy of that design and was made by a blacksmith in Verchères, Quebec, around the same time as the patent. Émile "Butch" Bouchard, a member of the Hockey Hall of Fame, contributed these to my collection. (Bouchard was a great collector of skates and, as I will discuss later, made some tremendous contributions to my collection.)

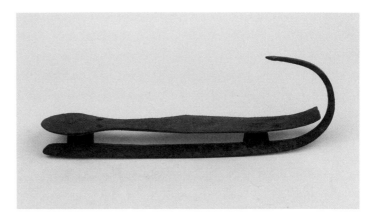

One of the reasons I like blacksmith skates is that I have a personal connection to them: my grandfather made skates, and I have a pair he created in 1921. He was a blacksmith in what is now Limoges, Ontario. He drilled holes in the footplate for the leather straps, so they are unlike the other blacksmith skates in the collection. These skates are also unique because the loop at the top of the blade is bigger than on a lot of other blacksmith skates, adding a bit of flair. As far as I know, my grandfather made twenty-two pairs of skates in his life. This is the only pair I've been able to track down, making them a particularly special part of my collection.

FOOTWEAR AND SKATES

Of course, the introduction of all-metal skates was not the only major development of the nineteenth century. The way skates were attached to people's feet also underwent a significant change. All the skates we have seen so far attached to the foot with either leather straps or adjustable clamps. But in 1826, the first pair of skates were produced that could be screwed directly into the skater's shoes. Placed at the heel and toe, the screws would ensure a tight connection between the foot and the skate.

ABOVE Canadian forestry staff, boots strapped to skates. Canada, ca 1919.

DEPT. OF NATIONAL DEFENCE/LAC

Once footwear was attached to a pair of skates, it was typically not removed. Older shoes or boots would have a second life on the ice. The process of attaching the blade was straightforward, as the screw in the skate went directly into the sole—no need to drill a hole first. Once the skate was attached properly, the boot would be permanently secured. Just as the clamps had done before, the skate was secured with a strong bond, thus allowing skaters to go faster without having to worry about slipping in their skates. These skates first came out in the first half of the nineteenth century, and their popularity really exploded in the decades that followed.

One pair from 1860 is a good example of how such screws work. It is a women's figure skate with a rounded nose at both the front and back of the blade. The screw at the back is quite prominent—a sign of how tight the connection to the foot could

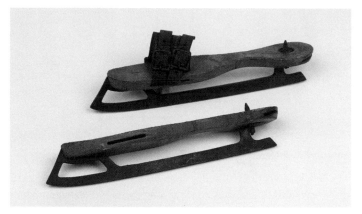

be—but there are also smaller screws in the middle and at the toes to ensure that no part of the boot comes dislodged from the footplate. A brass plate covers most of the top of the wood base, but at the heel there is a dip in the wood, which helps accommodate the larger screw for the thicker heel of the boot.

Another women's figure skate, from about ten years later, is an unusual design—so much so that I cannot positively identify the manufacturer, although certain signs suggest they were made by Union Hardware Co. Like the other pair, the long screw at the heel is visible, but unlike the other pair (and unlike a lot of screw-in skates), there are no screws at the toe. Instead, there is a slot in the beechwood base where a broad leather strap could be inserted and used to tie the front of the boot to the skate. To tighten the strength of the connection, the strap goes through a second slot by the screw.

THE RINK

The improvement in skates through the century was accompanied by another important change in skating: the quality of the ice. Until the late 1900s, skating was always done outdoors on natural ice. Not only were skating seasons shorter than they are now, but the blades had to withstand more than today's skates do. Natural ice tends not to be as smooth as artificial ice, so blades need to be sharpened more often and are more likely to be damaged. This started to change with the construction of arenas. The earliest arenas still used natural ice, but the shelter from the elements helped smooth the ice. In fact, the first indoor hockey game was played on natural ice in 1875 at Montreal's Victoria Arena, which opened in 1862.

Around the same time, there was another monumental development in the history of skating: the opening of Madison Square Garden in New York City. The Garden was the first arena in North America with a refrigeration unit, from which it produced artificial ice. Smoother, more consistent ice allowed skaters to tailor their skates for specific conditions, thus improving the overall quality of skating. It took time before artificial ice became common—it was not used at the Olympics until 1908 in London—because of limitations in electrical distribution and the cost of the equipment, but over time artificial ice began to replace natural ice as the most common surface for skating.

ABOVE "Quebec Skating Rink," 1860. Watercolour by E.J. MacGregor. LAC, ACC. NO. R9266-308/PETER WINKWORTH COLLECTION OF CANADIANA

As conditions improved and skates evolved, skaters could specialize in their preferred techniques and styles. These developments in the nineteenth century helped spark the growth of sports on ice. Where skating had long been used for communication, transportation, and recreation, now athletic competitions were organized. Whether they were games on ice or races to see who was the fastest, the skates of the nineteenth century paved the way for modern ice sports. The activity had grown to a global phenomenon, and now it was time to see who was the best. To do that, the skates needed to continue to improve.

F IGURE SKATERS HOLD a special place in this country's sports history. An athlete's combination of strength, flexibility, balance, and style can take an audience's breath away. Of course, it is possible to see all forms of skating as figure skating—or at least as part of ice dancing. Copley-Graves talks about "rhythmic skating" that is surely as old as gliding on skates, and says all forms of skating could be called dancing. Hockey, she argues, can be included as dance because its intricacies, the starts, stops, and twists, are all part of a rhythmic set of moves on the ice.

Of course, that romantic vision of skating does not entirely fit with the modern understanding of figure skating. It is generally thought that figure skating was born in England following the return of Charles II in 1660. Primarily an activity for distinguished gentlemen early on, the sport quickly grew in popularity as skaters became fascinated by the markings they could make in the ice with their skates, as Hines explains in *Figure Skating: A History*. And for a long time, figure skating remained an amateur pursuit in skating clubs around the world. But like other sports, figure skating began to be standardized in the nineteenth century, as competitors started to travel to compete against the best skaters other countries had to offer, mesmerizing crowds with their routines. The skates needed to improve and evolve as people pushed the limits of what began as a leisure activity. The sport has a hypnotic power, from the explosion of a quadruple Axel to the delicacy of intricate footwork—a power that comes directly from the skates.

Figure skates from the early nineteenth century do not look like modern figure skates. In fact, early figure skating was a more literal reflection of the name—skaters made figures on the ice. From figure eights to serpentines to hearts, these figures were required elements in routines until they were withdrawn following the 1990 world championships in Halifax. But as the equipment evolved, greater agility, stronger materials, and improved blades fundamentally changed the sport and allowed skaters to expand their repertoires.

Even though skates began to be manufactured in the nineteenth century with an eye toward specific uses, such as for playing hockey or speed skating, figure skates were slower to evolve. For the most part, skaters interested in figure skating were using skates that could also be used by hockey players. One pair from England, dating to the middle of the nineteenth century, has an unusual square platform at the toe that is more reminiscent of hockey skates than figure skates. In fact, these skates could have been used for a variety of purposes. The wood

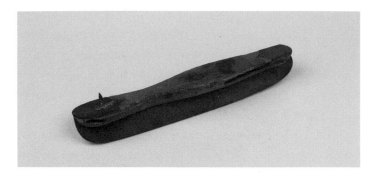

platform has a brass plate inlaid at the front and rear to improve the skate's strength. The runners are cast steel and curved at both ends, which helps the skater turn, a critical component when making figures.

An even better example of how skates for early figure skating were not specific to the sport is a pair from Starr Manufacturing in Nova Scotia, made in the 1860s. Called the "Falcon," this model could have been used by both hockey and figure skaters. Made of all steel, it was strong enough for the agility of hockey players and light enough for the speed of speed skaters. Like many figure skates, it has four stanchions that connect the runner to the heel and toe plates. The skate would then be attached to the skater's boot with screws. One of the key identifiers of this skate is the triangular tip at the front, which indicates that it was used for both hockey and figure skating. That shape was common in skate production at the time because of its versatility. Hockey players could get a quick start from a standing position, while figure skaters could use it to help them stop and make tight turns. While it was not ideal for either sport, at the time it worked for both sports.

ROUNDED FRONTS

Despite the popularity of these skates, figure skaters thought that a skate dedicated to their sport would improve their performance, which they hoped would then translate into greater adoption of the sport. A variety of ideas were discussed, but the one that really started to catch on was a skate with a rounded front. The design was simple—round off the front edge of the skate to allow for a smoother performance. Skaters were still focused on creating figures in the ice, so with the rounded front, they were less likely to trip on a point at the toe that characterized older skates. Skaters would then have more freedom to glide across the ice and perform more elaborate programs.

These skates started to appear in the 1860s. A good example of how this style was seen as an enhancement is in the name of a model produced in the second half of the 1880s, the "Engels

Improved Figure," manufactured in Ramscheid, Germany, by Edward Engels. The key difference between this pair and earlier figure skates is the rounded front extending above the toe plate. The back of the skate is also different, as the end of the blade does not come into the heel. An added benefit of this design is that it lengthens the blade beyond the foot, allowing for greater speed without inhibiting agility. While these skates are an early example of figure skates, they would not have been used for jumping. Athletes using these skates would have been exclusively creating figures in the ice, as the jumping that revolutionized figure skating had not quite caught on yet.

Fashion

FIGURE SKATERS ARE often recognized, in part, by their elaborate costumes—bright colours, sequins, drapery. While costumes these days may seem more ornate than they once were, figure skaters have always dressed boldly—and their skates had to fit the look. One pair in my collection, made in Germany by C.W. Wirths around the 1830s, is from a figure skate design used regularly from the late eighteenth to the early nineteenth century. The big loop at the toe is a dramatic feature with a practical purpose. Figure skaters, particularly men, wore long pants that hung over their toes and touched the ice, which would often lead to a fall. With this design, skaters could pull the cuff of their pants over the loop to ensure it never touched the ice. The fashion for such long pants faded, and so did the need for the toe loops. And while some skates retained the loop for aesthetic reasons, beginning in 1886 stop picks began to compete for space at the toe.

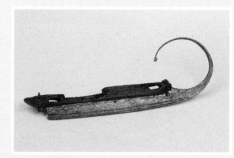

LEFT Orrin Markhus and Irma Thomas, figure skaters at the Ice Capades, Vancouver. 1962. PACIFIC NATIONAL EXHIBITION/CITY OF VANCOUVER ARCHIVES, 180-6265

RIGHT Handmade skate based on design by C.W. Wirths, German, ca 1830–1835. COLLECTION OF JEAN-MARIE LEDUC

STRENGTHENING THE BOND

The main problem with the rounded toe was that the front was too fragile. Without any support, the front of the blade was not as strong as it had been in the past. The blades were thus not as reliable, and given the amount of pressure figure skating puts on the toes, skaters wearing this model were not as confident in their skates. To resolve this problem, manufacturers started attaching the toe of the blade to a steel sole attached to a boot, which provided more support.

In the 1860s, Canadian manufacturers were some of the first to sell skates already attached to boots. Like earlier models, the "Acadie" skate by Starr, made for women, was used for both hockey and figure skating. Their real benefit was the thick blade, which made them very sturdy. The front point of the skate also helped skaters to start jumping, a critical development in the evolution of figure skating. The added stability made these skates heavier, but high-performance figure skaters seemed to prefer that to the fragility of rounded toes. More manufacturers, particularly those in the United States, began to produce skates already attached to boots.

Skaters liked this style, and many versions appeared. Around 1860, the American firm Barney and Berry made a skate with a chrome, nickel, and steel blade. The blade is long enough that it was also occasionally used for speed skating. Primarily a men's figure skate, the "Long Life," as it was known, is unique in that the blade is not as tall as on other models. While a critical element in speed skating, the height of a blade does not have the same significance in figure skating, but it does help this pair stand out from the rest. It is possible that the height of the blade could have been used for marketing purposes—a lighter blade would have appealed to skaters—at a time when the compulsory components of figure skating were changing, but it does not appear to have greatly influenced the performance of the figure skaters who wore this model.

TOP Women's
"Acadie" skates, Starr
Manufacturing Co.,
1860–1875. COLLECTION
OF JEAN-MARIE LEDUC

MIDDLE "Long
Life" skates,
Barney and Berry,
1860s. COLLECTION
OF JEAN-MARIE LEDUC

BOTTOM "Acadia" skate,
Starr Manufacuting Co.,
1860. COLLECTION OF
JEAN-MARIE LEDUC

When you watch figure skating today, so much of the outcome
is determined by jumps. Where figures used to be the only compulsory items, they have been replaced by a variety of moves, the
most important of which are the jumps. Axels, Salchows, Lutzes,
and toe loops must be mastered by anyone who dreams of becom-
ing a world champion. The legs of a figure skater are very strong,
like all skaters, but in a different way from those of speed skaters
or hockey players. Where a speed skater needs particularly strong
thighs, for example, a figure skater needs their entire legs and
body to be strong to complete routines that involve a variety of
motions and strides.

Central in that transition to a more physically challenging
routine was Jackson Haines, known to many as the father of figure skating. A ballet dancer by trade, Haines brought that style
to skating. He won a figure skating championship in the United
States in 1864, but moved to Europe after the event because
his style was not well received by audiences in his home country. He had great success in Vienna, where his combination of

ballet and figure skating resonated. While he invented a variety of spins, including the sit spin, he is best known for adding leaps and jumps to his routines. The style would not gain traction internationally until well after his death in 1875, but he had forever changed the sport.

Haines would not have been able to transform figure skating into a more athletic sport without the critical changes he made to his skates. When he first started, figure skaters were using leather straps to attach their skates to their feet. Haines found that this compromised his stability on the ice, and he wondered if there was a way to improve how the skates connected to the skater's feet. This was around the same time that manufacturers were experimenting with attached footwear with screws in the footplate, and Haines was one of the first athletes to use such skates. While some people argue whether he was the first to do so, he found wearing skates with blades that screwed directly into his footwear allowed him to make more intricate movements on the ice. This was because the skate, with a strengthened attachment to the foot, shifted less when skaters moved and was therefore more responsive. The tighter connection also created a more balanced distribution of weight between boot and skate. Haines was thus able to perform the acrobatic moves that have come to dominate modern figure skating.

Manufacturers eventually began to produce skates with boots already attached. In addition to the increased stability provided by attaching the boot directly, it was also a good marketing decision. Skaters were reluctant to ruin a pair of shoes by screwing a pair of skates into the sole, so selling skates already attached to a boot made a lot of business sense. Skaters liked the boot and blade combination and quickly adopted the new design. A good example of the functionality that came with boots is a pair produced in Halifax in 1860. Manufactured by Starr, these "Acadia" skates are one of the earliest examples of skates sold with boots attached. Connected by screws in three locations, these skates are similar to the ones Haines would have used in his performances. In addition to the stability that came with the blade–boot connection, the boot's height, initially a feature added for the protection of women's ankles when playing hockey, also provided support for elaborate jumping and twisting routines.

STOP PICKS

The ability to jump was greatly increased by the addition of stop picks, which came after Haines's time. These indentations on the front of the blade came to define figure skates in the twentieth century. The first pair of figure skates with stop picks were made in 1886 by CCM. The picks are valuable to figure skaters because they allow a skater to not only increase speed quickly from a standstill, but also, and perhaps more importantly, to stop instantly. Stopping to the side—where the skater puts pressure on the edge of their skate—takes time and space, something that is not always possible in a figure skating routine. The stop pick resolves this problem as skaters can simply dig their toes into the ice to stop. The next time you watch a figure skater, pay close attention to the toes and you will notice how often they use the picks to stop.

The more obvious way in which the picks are used is during jumps. Figure skaters perform both edge and toe jumps—the difference being the part of the skate that launches them into the air. Without stop picks, the toe jump, the toe loop, the flip, and the Lutz would not be possible. In all these jumps, as the skater is moving backwards, the picks are used to stop the athlete's momentum and leverage them into the air.

Stop picks revolutionized the sport, but they have changed substantially since their introduction. Originally, stop picks were

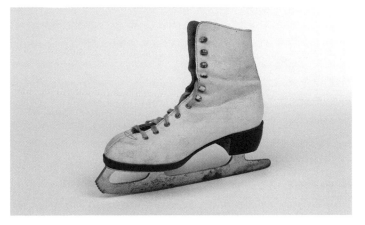

just notches in the blade. In a pair dating to 1915, made by Spalding of Swedish steel, the rounded front, which had been popular in the past, was back. In the toe of the blade are three notches. The round toe with picks allowed the skater to maintain speed throughout a routine. But while the notches allowed the skater to stop and perform jumps, they are still quite different from modern stop picks. In the "Gloria" figure skate from the 1980s, designed by Donald Jackson, who was also a world champion skater, the toe is given a much sharper angle and the pick is in a criss-cross pattern. There is more "pick" to the pick and it digs into the ice better. When combined with the improved angle of the toe relative to the ice, the pick gives the skater more leverage and more control of their movements.

The development of jumps in figure skating dramatically changed on-ice performance and helped increase the sport's popularity. A central figure in this development was Ulrich Salchow, the man who invented the jump that now bears his name. Born in 1877 in Stockholm, Sweden, Salchow, who would become a ten-time world champion, won the first Olympic gold medal for men's figure skating in London in 1908. Salchow was known for his generous spirit—he actually offered his 1902 world championship to a fellow competitor who he felt deserved the honour. His most enduring legacy, however, is the Salchow jump, which is generally considered the easiest in the sport. Skaters performing a Salchow take off from the rear inside edge of one skate and rotate in the air before landing on the outside edge of the other skate.

While Salchow helped bring attention to the sport, he was not its first major star. According to John Misha Petkevich in *The Skater's Handbook*, that honour goes to a Norwegian skater, Sonja Henie. A three-time Olympic champion, Henie was the most decorated skater of the inter-war period. Described in her obituary in the *New York Times* (October 13, 1969) as "a petite, glamorous woman with a taste for luxury and a shrewd business sense," she was a captivating skater and performer, charming audiences as she effortlessly glided across the ice. She had a long career both as a performing skater and as an actress. Setting the stage for future stars like Barbara Ann Scott, Henie showed that the advances in figure skating, made possible by the improved skates available just when she was ready for them, could expand the sport's popularity in unprecedented ways.

STURDY SKATES

While other ice sports were developing ways to lighten skates, the exact opposite happened in figure skating. To strengthen the boots and their connection to the blade, figure skates actually became heavier. It may seem counterintuitive for a sport where you have to launch yourself in the air, but as figure skaters started to experiment with triple and then quadruple jumps, manufacturers had to find ways to strengthen skates to withstand a great deal of force. Blades continued to be screwed directly into the boots so as to not compromise their strength and stability, and the boots were reinforced and the blades made thicker.

ABOVE Skate designed by J.C. Higgins, Canadian, mid-20th century. COLLECTION OF JEAN-MARIE LEDUC

A pair of skates made by J.C. Higgins around 1950 illustrates the added weight. The thicker leather on the sole, a heel made from several layers of compressed leather, and a reinforced boot make the skates very sturdy. They fit the image a lot of people have of women's figure skates. The blades are also noteworthy because they are of thick Sheffield steel, which further contributed to the skate's strength. Sheffield, a metropolitan area in South Yorkshire, earned a reputation for steel production in the nineteenth century. It did not take long for that reputation to extend to skate blades, and figure skaters all over the world wanted skates made of the strong Sheffield steel. Their quality is clear; when you look at them straight on, you can see how thick they are. They are strong, and even though they are over sixty years old, they look like they could still be taken out on the ice.

Barbara Ann Scott

A MODEL OF SKATE by CCM that has become the classic of figure skating, the Barbara Ann Scott skate, following her Olympic victory in 1948. In Ottawa's City Hall is a permanent exhibit celebrating the life and career of Barbara Ann Scott, the figure skating champion of the Winter Olympics held in St. Moritz, Switzerland. Scott was known as Canada's sweetheart for her graceful style and charming personality. She was a five-time Canadian champion, four-time North American champion, two-time Olympic and world champion, and three-time winner of the Lou Marsh Trophy as Canada's athlete of the year. In a country where hockey can overwhelm the national spotlight, Scott captured the national imagination and

ABOVE Barbara Ann Scott performing a Stag Jump at Minto Skating Club in Ottawa. 1947. FRANK ROYAL/
NATIONAL FILM BOARD OF CANADA/LAC, PA-112691

remained a revered Canadian icon—she carried the Olympic torch into the House of Commons in 2009—until her death in 2012.

I had the pleasure of meeting Barbara Ann during the opening of one of my exhibitions at the Canadian Museum of Civilization, now the Canadian Museum of History. I mentioned that I had been looking for a pair of her skates for years and she said, "I'll see what I can do." I figured that was a polite way of getting rid of me, but two years later, in 2011, I received a phone call from Georgette Grégoire, who lived in Montreal, asking if I still needed a pair of Barbara Ann Scott skates. She said she had a pair, which she had been using since 1956, that she could send to me and, sure enough, two weeks later the box arrived. Scott never used this pair herself, although her signature is on the blade. With blades made of Sheffield steel, they had been extensively used by the woman who gave them to me, who was a hockey player, figure skater, and barrel jumper. Because of the heavy usage, the screws in the heel needed to be replaced, but otherwise they are the original, dating to the 1950s. They are very heavy. When you think of Barbara Ann Scott, you think of her grace and beauty on the ice, but when you see these skates you realize just how strong she needed to be to complete her routines.

ABOVE "Barbara Ann Scott" model skates signed by the Olympic champion, 1950s. COLLECTION OF JEAN-MARIE LEDUC

While these skates were the standard through the second half of the twentieth century, a recent development provides greater flexibility for figure skaters: the ability to shift blades forward or backward depending on a skater's program. The full ramifications of this are still unknown, as athletes continue to experiment with the technology to determine the most effective way to position their blades. Like all other major developments in skates, this one reflects the athletes' demands for the best possible equipment.

Whether it was skates specifically for figure skating, rounded fronts, screwed-in blades, or toe picks, the evolution of figure skates has come from the skaters' desire to take their performance to the next level. If you were watching a figure skating competition from two hundred years ago, you would not recognize it—it is not the same sport today as it was then. There are many reasons for this—the athletes are better conditioned, the routines are more carefully planned, and the ice conditions are more consistent—but more important than any of these reasons are the skates. They allow the competitors to jump, spin, and perform in ways we never thought possible. And as figure skaters continue to push the limits of what is possible on the ice, more changes are certain to come.

WHILE THE BLADE of a figure skate has two edges to allow great agility, and is solid and heavy to withstand the impact when landing a jump, the blade of a speed skate developed in a different direction. It was soon recognized that a long blade was faster than a short one, and a thin blade without the double edge glided better through a long distance, but the added weight was a problem. Travelling on frozen lakes and rivers took time and effort, especially in cold weather. Anything that could be done to lighten a traveller's weight and increase their speed was welcome, and so manufacturers began to develop the precursors to the modern streamlined speed skate.

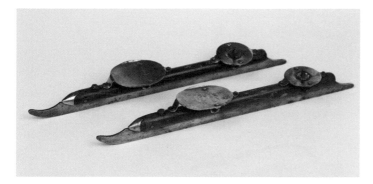

LEFT "Torpedo" speed skate by Raymond Skate and Bicycle Co., Boston, MA, ca 1866. COLLECTION OF JEAN-MARIE LEDUC

While many early skates designed for long distance and speed were generally made of iron, manufacturers experimented with a variety of materials. The pair in my collection with a long wooden dowel, to which both the steel blade and footplates are attached, was made by the Raymond Skate and Bicycle Company in Boston in 1866. Called "Torpedo" skates, they are longer and narrower than most skates of the time. Apart from that, however, they are very similar to the period's recreational skates. It was not until the last decade of the nineteenth century that manufacturers began to produce skates that were clearly meant for the sport of speed skating.

Speed skating, particularly short track, is relatively new. People have been racing on ice for hundreds of years, but there were no formal rules until Louis Rubenstein, a Canadian, came along. Most people know him for being a world champion figure skater, but he was also president of the International Skating Union and a prominent figure in many sports. In August 1886, with the establishment of Skate Canada, speed skating became a sport—in fact, speed skating and figure skating were the first two structured sports in Canada, under one association, and Hockey Canada was formed four months later. Rubenstein oversaw skating in Canada for a long time, and the sport grew in popularity.

Blades *with* Holes

O NE OF THE themes of skate design has long been how to reduce the weight of skates. Some manufacturers thought that removing pieces of metal from the blade was the solution. A pair from the late 1800s, possibly made by J.A. Whelpley, was used for long-distance skating. A screw in the heel would attach to the skater's boot, and the holes in the blade, which are quite large, take up most of the blade's height, leaving only a small band of steel at the top and bottom. This idea is copied from earlier skates, but the holes are even smaller, to account for the lower height of the blades used in skating long distances.

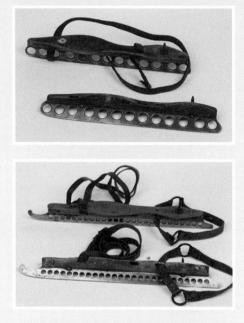

TOP Long-distance skate designed to reduce weight, possibly by J.A. Whelpley, Greenwich, NB, ca 1870S. COLLECTION OF JEAN-MARIE LEDUC

BOTTOM "Long Reach" skate by J.A. Whelpley, Greenwich, NB. COLLECTION OF JEAN-MARIE LEDUC

Whelpley made a less dramatic example around the same time for his brother William, who liked to skate on the St. John River but found his skates too heavy. Called "Long Reach," they are noticeably lighter than other pairs from this era, making them popular with some marathon skaters. The holes are not as large on this pair, leaving more steel at both the top and bottom of the blade, which maintains their strength. Ultimately, blades with holes were never widespread, but they were part of the trend toward the "tube" and the "Tuuk" (see Hockey chapter): skaters wanted lighter skates and were willing to try anything that made it easier on their legs.

THE TUBE

Good speed skating technique is all about aerodynamics. While a hockey player presses on their toes to get a quick burst of speed by extending each leg straight back, a speed skater presses on their heels and so extends each leg more to the side, creating continuous momentum as they skate and the characteristic sideways rocking motion. This is one of the reasons speed skaters stay crouched throughout a race. While that pose is more aerodynamic than skating upright, it also allows the leg to easily push out to the side and apply the necessary pressure to the heel. The skate also stays on the ice as long as possible, which is critical for building and sustaining speed. And the skate itself is critical to the overall aerodynamics.

The metal of a skate is its heaviest, and sometimes only, component. But cutting away metal to reduce weight can render a blade too low in height, and create difficulty turning—so it also cannot be shortened. Cutting holes into a taller blade was one solution, but not one that ever caught on. In the pursuit to reduce the weight of the blade, one of the most game-changing features emerged: "the tube." It dramatically changed the nature of skating quickly. A hollow length of metal within the blade, it was critical in reducing the weight of both hockey and speed skates. The development of the tube helped turn skating fast into an exciting sport of speed and skill.

One model, made in Remscheid, Germany, in the 1880s, was known as the "Polar-Racer," and is a predecessor to the type of innovation that came to be known as the tube. Remscheid is known for its mechanical engineering and metallurgic production, and they shaped a long hollow tube, egg-shaped on the bottom and flat on top, to attach to the blade. With the resulting reduction in weight, this model was designed for speed. The

TOP "Polar-Racer" skate, German, 1880s. COLLECTION OF JEAN-MARIE LEDUC

TOP, MIDDLE Speed skate, by Starr Manufacturing Co., late 1890s. COLLECTION OF JEAN-MARIE LEDUC

BOTTOM, MIDDLE Tube skate from Ted Barden, designed by Henry Boker, Canada, 1896. COLLECTION OF JEAN-MARIE LEDUC

BOTTOM "Cyco Speeder" skate, CCM, ca 1910. COLLECTION OF JEAN-MARIE LEDUC

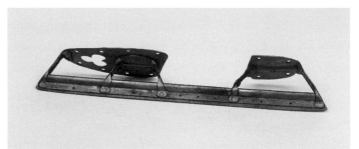

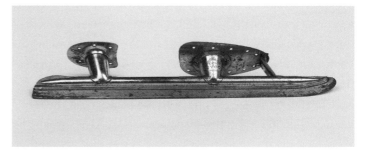

Germans were not the only ones experimenting, of course; Canadian companies also searched for ways to reduce the weight of a skate. In the 1890s, the Starr Manufacturing Company produced a skate that is very similar to the German design.

The problem, though, was that in reducing the weight, the blades lost some of their strength. To resolve that issue, the Germans continued to refine the tube concept. They inserted a circular hollow metal tube inside the blade. The circular shape would maintain the strength while using less metal, thus making the skate lighter. It was also important that any change made to the skates would not alter the way they functioned, so a critical part of the tube is that it provides equal pressure across the blade. Any imbalance in this would reduce a blade's effectiveness and compromise the skater's ability to generate speed. The tube quickly became standard in hockey and speed skates.

Many people believe that the first tube skates were made in 1906 for hockey, but as we shall see, tube skates appeared earlier in speed skating. World champions were skating on German tube skates in 1891. In addition, John "Jack" MacCollough, a skater from Winnipeg, reported seeing tube skates at a competition in 1896. One pair in my collection, produced around 1896, is one of the first examples of the tube skate. I actually obtained these skates from Ted Barden, a speed skater who received them from his father. He used them until he stopped skating in 1986 at age seventy-seven—you can tell how much he used them by the wear on the blades. The difference between these and the older skates is quite subtle, and lies in the shape of the tube: it is no longer flat on top but entirely round. The footplate is connected by five thin posts, another attempt to reduce the total weight of the skate. Of course, since the blade on these is quite short, they would not have been used by speed skaters, but they do show how the tube was used in the 1890s. You can see the holes along the outside of

RIGHT "Alamo" speed
skate, 1914. COLLECTION
OF JEAN-MARIE LEDUC

the footplate where the screws would be placed to attach to the skater's boot.

The "Cyco Speeder" has a longer blade, indicating that this model was used for speed skating. These skates were popular because of their reduced weight. It took a while for all companies to get on board with tubes—the "Alamo" speed skate from 1914 has no tube—but when skaters discovered their benefits, tubes became an essential feature for speed skates.

Barrel Jumping

IN BARREL JUMPING, several large plastic barrels are laid on the ice side-by-side, or sometimes on top of each other in a pyramid. One at a time, each skater, wearing speed skates, first does several laps around the rink, building speed, then jumps the line of barrels. They land on their backside. After each round, another barrel is added, and those who cleared the first distance try the new one.

Barrel jumping is not practised much anymore, but it once had quite a large following. In 1980 and 1981 during Winterlude in Ottawa, the Ottawa Pacers, the speed skating club of which I was a member, hosted a barrel jumping competition. Now, we were speed skating people, so we did not know exactly whom we should invite to compete, and we ended up with an eclectic group of participants. With people from around Canada and Europe, the competitors ranged from those who had never jumped barrels before to the world champion. Most of the experienced jumpers were able to clear sixteen barrels, but the world champion, Giles Leclerc, a French-Canadian from Montreal, was able to jump eighteen, a record that still holds today.

The CCM speed skates that belonged to André Carrière, given to me by his grandson, were used exclusively for barrel jumping. Made in the 1920s or 1930s, one of them has a protector from the tip of the blade to the front of the boot, a safety requirement. Like other speed skates at that time, the blades are steel with a tube. To land on the backside, the body needs protection, but the skates do not need to be reinforced or strengthened; their primary function is to go fast.

TOP Sylvain Leclerc barrel jumping, Terrebonne, Ile-des-Moulins, Quebec, 2012. COURTESY MARIE FRANCE GIARD AND SYLVAIN LECLERC

BOTTOM CCM speed Speed skates used for barrel jumping, once owned by André Carriere, 1920s or 1930s. COLLECTION OF JEAN-MARIE LEDUC

SKATES THAT FIT

After the introduction of the tube, speed skates did not change much through the first half of the twentieth century. Once manufacturers universally used tubes in their designs, they could not see much that could be changed. By the 1960s, however, there was a sense that there was room for improvement. The Dutch company, Viking, founded by celebrated speed skater Jaap Havekotte, was the next great innovator. Havekotte began his business by sharpening skates, then went into repairs, and eventually produced marathon skates—with a new focus on the fit of the boots. Just as it seems fitting that Germany produced a major innovation in the metal of skates, it seems right that a Dutch company became the primary producer of speed skates around the world. Speed skating is the national sport in the Netherlands— they can fill 20,000-seat arenas for national competitions—and Viking was always looking for ways to improve speed skates and, by extension, the sport. Ironically, the first person to win a medal at a major competition on Viking skates was not Dutch; it was a Russian, Boris Stenin, who won a bronze medal in the 1,500 metre at the 1960 Olympics in Squaw Valley.

Speed skaters want boots that are tailored to their feet, which is exactly what Viking produced. One of the earliest pairs Havekotte designed are long-distance skates with blades made from polished steel. Originally purchased in 1962, they came to my collection from Dutch marathon skater Peter van Musschenbroek in 1988. Renowned for the fit of their boots, Viking developed different designs, usually of tanned leather. Their boots were so well made that, over time, a pair in your size could mould to your feet, feeling eventually like they were tailor-made. Clara Hughes has written that her first pair of Viking skates, which she bought second hand, fit her like a glove.

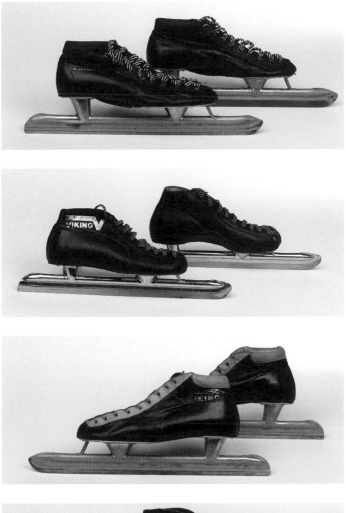

TOP Long-track speed skate, Viking, Dutch, 1960s. COLLECTION OF JEAN-MARIE LEDUC

TOP, MIDDLE Long-track speed skate, Viking, Dutch, early 1960s. COLLECTION OF JEAN-MARIE LEDUC

BOTTOM, MIDDLE Marathon skate, Viking, Dutch, 1960s. COLLECTION OF JEAN-MARIE LEDUC

BOTTOM "Junior" speed skate, Viking, Dutch. COLLECTION OF JEAN-MARIE LEDUC

Another benefit of the Viking boot is that the front is cut low, a key design element. The pair from my collection made sometime in the 1960s has an opening at the top and front of the boot, which allows the skater to bend their lower shin forward while they skate. Viking produced many different models, from "Junior" skates to ones simply stamped "Havekotte #26." Viking remains the most popular brand for Olympic and world championship speed skaters, primarily because of the company's high quality and their capacity for innovation, constantly looking for ways to improve their skates.

Gaétan Boucher

GAÉTAN BOUCHER'S SKATES came to me through my involvement with speed skating. In 1987 I was putting together a promotion for the Olympics in Calgary, so I called Gaétan and asked him if I could have a pair of his skates. I had known him since 1976, but with the Olympics coming up—he was very busy because short track had been included as a demonstration sport—he referred me to his manager. A couple of weeks after talking with his manager I received a box with a pair of skates and a note saying this was the pair he used to win his gold medals at the 1984 Olympics in Sarajevo. I was shocked—I thought he might send a pair that he used for training, so to get the skates he used in the competition was a real prize. The skates themselves are a typical pair of Viking sprint skates from the 1980s, but what they helped achieve was remarkable.

TOP Gaétan Boucher competes in Alkmaar, Netherlands, February 6, 1982. NATIONAAL ARCHIEF (NETHERLANDS)

BOTTOM Short-track speed skates by Viking, worn by Gaétan Boucher, 1980s. COLLECTION OF JEAN-MARIE LEDUC

CUSTOM-MADE QUALITY

While Viking continues to make the most popular brand, the company is far from the only major innovator in speed skates. One of the most important innovators was Bob Planert. He worked for Bauer in Chicago and was responsible for making both speed skates and sharpening jigs. Even though Planert worked for such a big company, his skates were known for being handmade using the best materials available. He was obsessive about his skates. When Bauer moved their production facility to Cambridge, Ontario, it quickly became the centre for manufacturing speed skates in North America. Planert would slave over every detail of each pair of skates to ensure they met the skater's requirements. A soft-spoken and gentle man, he was easy to work with and skaters came to love his approach to making skates.

Planert had the same standards for his hockey skates. A hockey player came to him once to ask if he could raise and shorten the toe in his boots—he felt that if his toes were curled in the front of the skate he could put more pressure on the blade and go faster. Planert took a cast of the skater's foot in that position and handcrafted a boot. He was a genius at skate design and his designs were a popular choice among top athletes—so popular, in fact, that he worked until he was eighty years old before finally retiring, in the early 1980s. He was also a starter for speed skating—he had a reputation for being very strict with false starts. When he finally had the time to make it to the Olympics himself, though, his Olympic glory was seeing his skates on the feet of many Olympic champions.

Skaters throughout North America wanted Planert's skates. In addition to the handcrafted and personalized boots, Planert changed blades in a major way. Because speed skaters are always making left turns on the ice, Planert decided to put the blade on the left side of the boot. Doing this would allow skaters to lean

LEFT "Planert Special"
speed skate, Bauer, late
1960S. COLLECTION OF
JEAN-MARIE LEDUC

into the turn more than when the blade was under the centre
of foot, thus putting more pressure on the skates and enabling
them to go faster in the turns. This does make straight-aways
a little harder—you would never skate a marathon in these
skates—but for speed skating these offset blades marked a major
improvement.

The "Planert Special" demonstrates how the blade has moved
to the left of the boot. This particular pair was worn by Gerry
Cassan of Ottawa in 1974 when he won a 500-metre race in
Davos, Switzerland. These skates are quite meaningful to me,
not only because they represent a major shift in skate design, but
because Bob Planert was a good friend of mine, as was Gerry Cassan. I met Planert at speed skating competitions and we talked
about skates. He was very knowledgeable. His story demonstrates
how one person can singlehandedly change a sport.

BLADE SHARPENING

One thing that Planert could not change—that no one has been
able to change—is the need to sharpen the blades. Sharpening
skates can be a laborious task, especially when done by hand, but
it is vital for skating. Speed skaters cannot take their skates to

get sharpened at the local sports store or the arena pro shop. The blade of a speed skate is thinner than that of a figure skate or hockey skate, so that the blade can dig into the ice with greater efficiency and does not compromise the strength required for speed skating. In hockey and figure skating, the blade is put under much more pressure than in speed skating because of sudden changes in direction, but when you are doing laps, the pressure is consistent, so a thinner blade can support the skater.

That is not to say that a thin blade is weak. The history of skates for racing is full of experiments with material that is both strong enough and light enough, while also meeting the other demands of use on ice. Older blades were made from iron, but the weight made that unsustainable. Today's blades are made from chrome or stainless steel. Manufacturers have tried other metals like titanium, but they have proved too brittle for skates. Sometimes the metals are combined in the blade, while other times the chrome is layered on top of the steel. This occasionally leads to the chrome peeling off. And while that helps identify the blades, it goes to show how difficult it can be to preserve them. What you want in a blade is something that is not only strong and can handle constantly being wet, but also has a little flexibility. With the amount of pressure they are under and the constant bumps they take, blades have to be able to withstand a lot without being destroyed. This is why stainless steel and chrome are so popular—they do not rust and can take a lot of punishment. Even though the blades are thin, it would take a lot to break one. An even stronger blade that would never rust, in my opinion, is one made with four metals—stainless steel, nickel, chrome, and copper.

However, thin blades must be sharpened by hand. No machine in the world can properly sharpen speed skates, and that's not just because of how thin they are. The edge required on speed skates is different than the edge required on other skates. In speed skating, because you are only going in one direction, you want a ninety-degree angle on the edge, going from the inside to the outside of the blade. At the same time, blades today are bent ever so slightly to the left to further improve speeds in the turns. These improvements allow the blade to dig into the ice more effectively than a hockey or figure skating blade. Of course, such a blade would never be used in those sports because you would never be able to stop—notice how gingerly speed skaters approach the starting line so as to not wear down the edge—and you would never be able to go backwards.

Just as skaters prefer boots that accommodate the peculiarities of their own feet, skaters have distinct preferences in how their skates are sharpened, which is why so many people sharpen

TOP Sharpening jig, Spalding, 1926. COLLECTION OF JEAN-MARIE LEDUC

MIDDLE Sharpening jig, Bauer-Planert, Kitchener, ON, 1970. COLLECTION OF JEAN-MARIE LEDUC

BOTTOM Sharpening, jig, Joha Overbeke, Den Haag, Netherlands, 1985. COLLECTION OF JEAN-MARIE LEDUC

their own skates. At competitions, most skaters will warm up and then sharpen their skates before the race to tailor the skates to the ice conditions on that day. Skaters tend to travel with sharpening jigs, which in the past were often made of wood, but today are metal. Their purpose is to hold the skate in place while it is being sharpened, with a sharpening stone. The stones vary depending on how sharp the skater wants the blade, but the key is to eliminate burrs along the edge that would compromise the blade's effectiveness. Therefore, the last thing done when sharpening is to run a burr stone along the blade to ensure the perfect edge. The skater has to pay attention when doing this because not only do they want the perfect edge for the race, but the blades can be dangerous. As careful as the skater may be, bad things can happen around such thin and sharp blades. At one competition where I was announcing, a skater's hand slipped when he was sharpening his skates and he cut both wrists. One hand was in a cast for six months and the other for three or four weeks.

At the end of a race, Christine Boudrias, a two-time Olympic medallist for Canada in short-track speed skating, got her skate caught with another skater and fell, her leg slashed. She slid toward the boards, leaving a trail of blood on the ice. Fortunately, one of the coaches, who was also a physician, immediately wrapped the leg with the referee's jacket. The slash severed an artery, requiring 123 stitches. For a lot of people, this would have been the end of their career. Despite warnings that she may never walk without a limp, let alone skate at a championship level, Christine was determined to get back on the ice, telling her coach that she would make the Olympic team. Not only did she stun everyone by making the team, but she won a medal.

The subtleties of the rocker is another aspect to consider when sharpening skates. The rocker is the contour of the edge of the blade in relation to the horizontal ice. The rocker on a hockey or figure skate is bigger than on a speed skate—there is more contour in the blade. When a hockey player or figure skater stands straight with their feet flat, only a portion of the blade is in contact with the ice. That shape in the blade—the rocker—makes it easier to stop, turn, and go backwards. In speed skating, where you do not have to stop, turn, or go backward, the rocker is much smaller; when a speed skater stands straight up, more of the blade is in contact with the ice. This is not only because hockey players and figure skaters need to be more agile on their skates, but also because more contact with the ice increases speed, so a larger rocker could slow a speed skater down.

Getting the perfect rocker is a tough job and can take upwards of an hour. While most skaters have them done by experts, world-class speed skaters tend to do it themselves, recognizing that the perfect rocker could be the difference that gets them on the podium. In 2005, a new and efficient rocker machine came on the market and is often bought by skating clubs.

Skaters have to learn from the best if they are going to maintain their own skates. In Ottawa, one of the best was John Graham, a master of skate maintenance. From sharpening to drying skates to avoid corrosion, John knew everything there was to know about the proper care of skates. He also invented a great skate guard. Using pennies as rivets, John connected a piece of thick leather to a piece of air tube from a tire to hold the skate in place. These were by far the most effective guards I have ever come across. And while John was renowned for his maintenance, his whole family was involved in skating: John was also a starter, his wife was a timer, and his daughter and three sons were successful skaters.

VARIATIONS IN ICE

One thing skaters cannot control is the surface on which they are skating. While indoor speed skating is quite different from outdoor skating because indoor ice is manufactured, the ice can still vary considerably, depending on the arena. Warm temperatures and higher humidity lead to softer ice than colder temperatures and lower humidity. Softer ice is more difficult to skate on—it can feel sluggish to a skater, because the friction of the blades on the ice does not easily generate the water they need to glide on the ice. This is because the blade will dig into the ice rather than slide on top. Of course, it is not just the weather that affects the quality of the ice; the water is a major factor. When making ice, the water should be clear and clean. The dirtier the water, whether cloudy or full of pigments, the worse the ice will be because it has a more difficult time freezing. The purer the water, the purer the ice, and the purer the skating conditions.

In speed skating, skaters tailor their skates to the ice conditions. Depending on the conditions, they may need to change the edge or the rocker or even the blade, so it is important to know in advance exactly what type of ice the competition will be held on. Given weather variations around the world, it is impossible to have a universal standard in the temperature and humidity of arenas, so skaters need to adjust wherever they go. To prevent too much of a home-ice advantage, the referees monitor the ice to make sure it stays at the same temperature from the start of warmups through the end of the competition. Some hosts used to change the conditions after all skaters warmed up, so that only their skaters would be prepared for the type of ice they would skate on during the event. Now, throughout a competition, ice technicians will scan the ice with handheld monitors to ensure the temperature does not change. And if something is off, the competition is immediately stopped by the referee until they can ensure everything is fair. Such problems are rare now, though, as ice-making technology is so sophisticated that high-level competitions are, for the most part, contested on perfect ice. The oval in Richmond, BC, which was used during the 2010 Olympics, produced some of the best ice speed skaters have seen.

However, even when the skates are sharpened perfectly and the conditions are ideal, other things can go wrong with skates. During a competition in Ottawa, for instance, I was announcing the 400-metre race and someone found a nut on the ice. I made an announcement and Larry Magloire came over and said, "That's from my skate!" During the race he had noticed that his blade felt loose but did not know why. The next year at the same competition, we found a screw on the ice. I made an announcement and, once again, Magloire came over and said, "That's from my skate!" For years after this, whenever I saw him at competitions— he became a coach—I would always ask him, "Have you lost your screws?" It is a good example of what can happen when you do not pay enough attention to the condition of your skates.

SHORT-TRACK SUBTLETIES

In this discussion about speed skates so far, it has mostly been about long-track speed skates. Long-track speed skating—on 400-, 333-, or 220-metre tracks and, for the most part, with only two skaters at a time—has been an Olympic event since 1924 (it was scheduled to be included in the 1916 Olympics, which were cancelled due to the First World War). Short-track speed skating, on the other hand, is relatively new, with the first world championships being held in Meudon-la-Forêt, France, in 1981. One of the reasons for this is that no skates were made just for short track until the 1980s. Before that, people would compete in short track, but the skates were not designed for it and competitions were not Olympic quality. If you think short track is like a roller derby now, you should have seen what it was like before they had specialized skates. People fell a lot and races were too often decided not by who was the best skater but by who could stay on their feet. This is because in short-track races, unlike long track, several skaters are all racing against each other at the same time, and not against the clock. This makes the race exciting. It also leads to lots of contact, and because the track is shorter, skaters also spend more times in the turns, and so there are more oppor- tunities to crash.

Everything changed when Raymond Laberge began experi- menting with skates specifically for short-track racing. Laberge was a skater on Canada's national team, and he wanted to develop a skate specifically for short-track races. Working in Quebec City

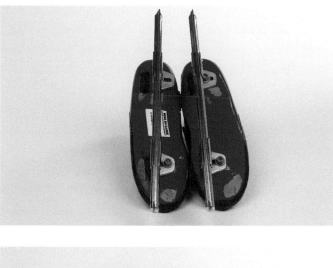

in the early 1980s, he asked Maryse Perreault and Louis Grenier
to try out his ideas. Over the course of a couple of years, Laberge
produced several prototypes while Perreault and Grenier provided feedback and made suggestions. At one point, Grenier
wondered if they could offset the blade in the tube. The tube was
already quite small in speed skates, so room to move the blade
was minimal—just a millimetre or two. And with the blades
already offset on the boot, it was not clear how much difference

moving the blade would make. Grenier estimated, however, that he could gain as much as three-tenths of a second in the corners with the change, which, in speed skating, can be the difference between first and last place. It was that attention to detail that characterized Laberge's testing process.

They made plenty of subtle changes to the skates, but the one that ultimately changed the sport was Laberge's idea to increase the height of both the blades and boots. Just like offsetting the blades, increasing their height gives the skaters more room to lean into the turns. This not only lets them go faster, but reduces the risk of a skater's boot touching the ice, which reduces the number of falls in a race. The skates were first used in competition in 1983, and it was quickly apparent that they were more superior for short-track skating than any other skates ever produced. As word of this development spread, more and more skaters used Laberge skates in competition. They became so popular that he told me he was guaranteed to win a gold medal at the 1993 world championships. Confused, I asked if he was returning to competition. He replied, "No, all the skaters are wearing my skates."

In my collection is one of the early versions of these skates. Made in 1982 or 1983, this model is responsible for changing short-track speed skating. It may be difficult to see when looking at the skates on their own, but there is a noticeable difference in height. That extra space proved vital in races and allowed the sport to move away from the perception that it was simply roller derby on ice. Another major benefit of these blades is that they are adjustable—both sideways and from back to front. And not only are the blades offset on the boot, but they are also offset in the tube. That this idea came from Louis Grenier should not be surprising as he inherited great insight into the sport from his father, who was influential in shaping its rules. Blue on the boots tells us that they were not customized, while customized pairs were given a red heel. Because they were so popular, Laberge had to hire students from Université Laval to help with their production.

Over the years, plenty of attempts have been made to make it easier for skaters in the turns and reduce the number of crashes. One innovation has been to put a slight curve in the blade of the skate for this type of racing. By bending the blade to the left, the skates naturally want to go that way, which really helps in the turns. The bend is not pronounced, and can be made by gently pounding a rubber hammer on the blade. Today, a machine is usually used because of its greater precision in meeting the requirements of each skater. Because a short-track race is won and lost on the turns, this can really help a skater gain an edge over the competition.

One of the most important rules of speed skating relates to the dimensions of the oval track. Short-track speed skating in the Olympics is held on a track created on the same rink generally used in figure skating. Over the years there have been a variety of tracks—most notably the double radius, which was a 100-metre oval—but now they race on tracks that are 111.12 metres. One of the benefits of racing on a track of this length is that each racer can start at a different spot on the ice while the finish line stays on the same side. The five starting positions are a metre apart and, for the most part, two races would begin from the same spot before changing. The ice is marked at both ends, which allows the corner block volunteers to shift the cones from both ends in the same direction after two races, and skaters are always on fresh ice. At the referee's discretion, the entire ice might be resurfaced several times throughout a competition. This is just one of many steps to save the ice quality. Another is spreading water on the track periodically throughout the competition to repair the ice, so programs can easily jump from 500-metre races to 5,000-metre races without too much ice damage.

As skaters flocked to Laberge skates, short-track speed skating improved greatly. The number of crashes decreased and times improved. The ultimate goal for those involved in the sport was to have it included in the Olympic program. It had its chance to prove itself at the 1988 Olympic Games in Calgary, when it was a demonstration sport. Demonstration sports are not common anymore at the Olympics—there have been none in the Winter Olympics since 1992—but host committees can include them in the schedule to help promote a sport and show the International Olympic Committee that they are worthy of being a medal sport. That is what happened with short track following 1988; it made its Olympic debut in Albertville, France, in 1992.

With its status as an Olympic sport, short track grew in popularity, which scared some folks in Canada, who thought we might lose our place as the best in the world. The Canadian women's relay team quelled those fears, however, winning nine consecutive world championships. Over those years, other countries challenged the Canadian women's team—the first time the Canadians won, they were miles ahead of the second-place team—but the Canadians would not easily cede their spot as the best in the world. While the roster changed every year, with mainstays like Isabelle Charest, Christine Boudrias, Sylvie Daigle, and Nathalie Lambert, it is not surprising that the Canadian team had such a prolonged period of success. I had been in contact with Canada Post about making a stamp to commemorate those nine consecutive championships, but unfortunately, with a change in the administration of Speed Skating Canada, the idea was forgotten. Nine consecutive world championships will likely never happen again.

MARATHON SKATES

One of the things that most people do not know about speed skating is that in addition to long and short track, there is also marathon skating. These are outdoor races on frozen lakes, rivers, and canals. A few marathon races have been held in Ottawa—once a skater became lost after a fall and got turned around, returning to his last check point—and they are quite popular in the Netherlands. The Dutch put straw between the frozen irrigation canals, where marathons are held, so that skaters can walk from one canal to another.

Some people like to use long skates with bases to which they can attach their own footwear, while others prefer skates with boots attached. One thing is certain, though: you would not want to wear short-track skates for a marathon. Because they are not designed for turns, they would hurt your feet. As I always tell people, you would not go running in high heels, so why go skating with the wrong skates?

ABOVE Speed skaters crossing over straw to a different canal in Harlingen, during Elfstedentocht, the Eleven Cities Tour, through the frozen canals of Freisland. February 21, 1985. SJAKKELIEN VOLLEBREGT/ANEFO/ NATIONAAL ARCHIEF (NETHERLANDS)

One pair of Dutch skates in my collection, made in the 1970s by J. Nooitgedast, is a good example of marathon skates. The key differences between these and short-track skates is that not only are the blades centred on the boot, but they are also lower to the ice. In addition, the taper in the blades is different, which was an innovation introduced by Bob Planert. He would taper about a ten thousandth of an inch off outdoor skates, creating a blade that was slightly thinner in the back. Because the back of the blade glides over the moisture created by the front, it does not need to be as thick. So by tapering the blade, there is less friction toward the skater's heel, which helps them go faster. In short, his skates make it easier to go a long distance because they are specifically designed to go straight.

CLAP SKATES

Tapered blades and shorter skates are examples of subtle changes that make a big difference in speed skating. The biggest improvement to speed skates, however, is also the most noticeable. If you ever walk into a speed skating oval, the most prominent sound you will hear is a continuous clapping. That is not applause, it is the skates, and this clapping is the most significant change to

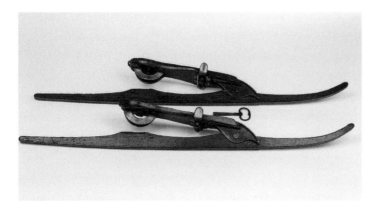

speed skates we have ever seen for long track. The design is simple—a spring in the footplate allows the heel to come up, making the clapping sound, while the blade remains on the ice. The longer the blade is in contact with the ice, the faster you can go.

It was not an original idea, though. Clap skates, as they are known, appeared at least as early as the late 1800s. In my collection is a pair from Montreal that was made in 1871. George-Étienne Cartier, one of the Fathers of Confederation, received a pair just like this from his wife as a Christmas gift in 1873. The elongated skis tell us that they were river skates and had to navigate both ice and snow. The elevated footplates feature a screw at the heel that attaches to the skater's shoes, while the clamps at the front are tightened with a key. The footplate is hinged to the blade beneath the toes, so that when a skater starts to pick up the foot to move forward, the heel rises but the toe stays down, allowing the blade to stay on the ice longer than it does with regular skates. The clapping sound is made when the toe comes off the ice, thus forcing the heel, fitted here with a metal bracket and spring, back to the footplate. That metal bracket keeps the footplate aligned above the blade and also prevents any wood-on-wood contact, helping to preserve the wood.

The first time I saw a modern clap skate was in Leeuwarden, Netherlands, in 1983. I was with the president of the Dutch speed skating association after a competition when we stopped in Heerenveen at the oval, where I kept hearing a clapping noise coming from the ice. They were testing an early prototype. Once their design had been worked out, clap skates became essential to any long-track speed skater. Speeds increased from around 50 kilometres an hour to upwards of 61 kilometres. World records are being shattered as skaters continue to push for faster times.

Despite the effectiveness of clap skates, some skaters were reluctant to adopt them. They require a different skating technique, which takes time to develop. Because the blade is on the ice while the heel is coming up, the motion of bringing the foot forward needs to change, especially at the start. And by going faster, a different number of strides are taken to get around the track. I remember Catriona Le May Doan telling her coach that she could not use them, only to be convinced when she realized that if she did not use them she had no chance of winning. Skaters who did not grow up on clap skates have to adapt to the new technology if they want to stay competitive. However, clap skates are not used in short track, for safety reasons. Even though crashes are less frequent now than they used to be, the possibility of blades getting tangled and doing serious damage is enough to keep clap skates out of short-track skating.

The changes to skates in speed skating have affected the sport more than changes to skates in any other sport. Skaters are going faster than ever before on the long track, and the short track is one of the most exciting sports to watch, with relays featuring up to sixteen skaters competing for position on the ice at the same time. In short track, skaters compete against each other, rather than against each other's times, like they do in long track. That is changing, however, as mass-start long-track races, where all skaters start at the same time, will be included at the Olympics in 2018. Long-track races with a mass start have been held in the Olympics before—the North Americans dominated the competition at the 1932 games in Lake Placid because they were accustomed to mass start, while it was new to the Europeans. It will be exciting to see it back in the Olympics as another sign of the sport's growth. From iron skates to the tube to offset blades to the clap skate, speed skates have evolved in a way that has revolutionized the sport. For all the talk about new aerodynamic suits and techniques, it really comes down to the sport's essence: the blade on the ice.

Engineering Experiment

OF ALL THE unique pairs in the collection, one of my favourites comes from students at the engineering department at Université Laval in Quebec City. When you look at them from the side, they look like normal skates, but when you turn them over, the blade is unlike anything you have ever seen. A regular blade is in contact with the ice on two edges. This skate has four edges because a slot between the two sides adds two extra inner edges. The hope was that it would increase a hockey player's speed or versatility. With four edges, the skates, in theory, would be more responsive to sharp turns and stops. Unfortunately, the innovation did not work that way and the skate was never produced on a large scale. Even though the skate is considered a failure, it shows ingenuity and how people continue the push to improve skates and the sports in which they are used. This pair came to me from Pierre Jury of *Le Droit*.

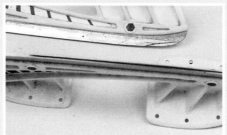

ABOVE A double-edged blade design for hockey skates, by engineering students at Université Laval, inserted into base made by PFZ Enterprises in Montreal, Quebec, 1977. COLLECTION OF JEAN-MARIE LEDUC

PLAYING HOCKEY REQUIRES both speed and agility. At an exhibition to showcase the skills of both speed skating and hockey, Gaétan Boucher, a double gold medallist in speed skating at the 1984 Olympics, was matched with a hockey player from the Vancouver Canucks. They both attempted the same drills from each of the sports. Gaétan was no match for the hockey player in navigating obstacles with a stick and puck, and he wasn't even close when they were skating backwards. But skating laps was a different story. They lined up, and the hockey player took off, but Gaétan remained at the starting line. The hockey player completed one lap. Not a move from Gaétan. Two laps. Not yet. Three laps. Gaétan took off just as the hockey player began to get tired. The hockey player was going about eight miles an hour, but with his speed skates Gaétan could go thirty. So even though the hockey player had a three-lap head start, Gaétan won the race. Both were great athletes, but it all came down to the types of skates they were wearing and what those skates allowed them to accomplish.

LEFT New skates.
LAC/NATIONAL
FILM BOARD FONDS/
E011176444

Hockey skates are probably the most versatile of all skates, and hockey players the most agile of skaters. While in figure and speed skating, the effect of a skater's movements on their skates is planned in advance, hockey players have to be able to stop on a dime, make quick, unanticipated turns, and rapidly switch from one edge of their skates to the other. That is what happened during the hockey player versus speed skater exhibition; the hockey player easily won anything related to agility. Like in other sports, though, to attain such a high level of function, hockey skates had to undergo a series of changes first. In certain cases, hockey has adopted advancements in skates from other sports, but most of the time the improvements have been in response to the needs of players. As the sport has become faster and the players bigger and stronger, the skates have had to keep up—which inspires many Canadians to continue to watch hockey on Saturday nights during the winter.

"Butch" Bouchard

BECAUSE OF MY involvement in speed skating and putting together this collection of skates, I have had the great fortune to meet some of Canada's winter sports legends. Of all of them, one in particular has had a tremendous influence on my collection. I first met Émile "Butch" Bouchard in Montreal during one of the exhibitions of this collection. I asked him if he still had his skates, and while he said he did, he did not seem too interested in contributing to the collection. The next time I saw him was in Montreal during an exhibition at the McCord Museum to commemorate the centenary of the

ABOVE Émile "Butch" Bouchard in 1945. ICEHOCKEY-WIKIA.COM

Stanley Cup. This time he was more intrigued and told me to come to his house to see his skates. When I got there, he had sixty-six pairs laid out on a table in his basement. The pair that really caught my eye was the original wood clap skate that I had been in search of for twelve years, but he said it was all or nothing. It took me six years to get the money to purchase all sixty-six pairs. (I was finally able to acquire them thanks to Jasmin Simard, owner of the Figure 8 boutique in Ottawa, who fronted the funds, without which I may not have been able to acquire them.)

ABOVE "Prolite" skates by CCM, worn by Emile "Butch" Bouchard, ca 1961. COLLECTION OF JEAN-MARIE LEDUC

ABOVE "Tacks Prolite" skates by CCM, worn by Pierre Bouchard, early 1970s. COLLECTION OF JEAN-MARIE LEDUC

When I went to his house to pick up the skates I noticed two extra bags by the door. When I asked about them, Butch said one bag had two pairs of his skates, while the other had his son's, all of which had been used during the respective tenures of father and son with the Montreal Canadiens. He said, "They're yours if you want them." A couple of days later I got a call from the Hockey Hall of Fame, asking me how I got the skates and why he gave them to me. I could not reveal the real reason, as that will stay between the two of us, so I just told them to ask Butch. One is the CCM "Prolite" model, which were purchased later in his life—the plastic guard on the heel dates it to around 1961. The blades are made entirely of steel. This model is actually quite similar to his son Pierre's skates, which are the CCM "Tacks Pro-lite" model and were made perhaps ten years later. The two are so similar that it is some-times difficult to tell them apart, and while they actually say "Butch" on the inside, these are smaller than Butch's skates. Even though the skates are not of particularly notable design, these pairs from a Hall of Famer are popular at my exhibitions.

RECREATION TO FORMAL SPORT

ABOVE Open rink in Riverdale, Toronto, Ontario, December 30, 1915. Photo by John Boyd. JOHN BOYD/LAC

Like other sports on ice, hockey began to evolve into a formal sport with standardized rules around the middle of the nineteenth century. Of course, games resembling hockey have been played for hundreds of years, but the version we see today is quite young. James Creighton, a young man who moved from Halifax to Montreal, is generally credited with bringing hockey west from the Maritimes. He also organized the first indoor game at the Victoria Arena in Montreal in 1875. The biggest development with which he is credited is the invention of the puck. Before this, teams would use lacrosse balls, often cut in half to lie flat on the ice. Creighton created a puck out of wood, which was easier to pass and shoot. This allowed the players' skills to shine and helped the sport grow in the latter part of the nineteenth century—along with the evolution of skates.

The critical factors that make a skate ideal for hockey are the rocker and blade length. With a short rocker, a hockey player can turn quickly, and with a short blade, movements are efficient. It is nearly impossible to skate backward on long blades because the blades get in the way of the body's movements. While the pressure when wearing speed skates is on the heels, speed skates are not designed for skating backwards where the pressure on the ball and toes of the foot. But these special refinements took time to develop.

As we have seen, early skates were often heavy and bulky, making it difficult for the skater to make quick moves. That all changed when the Starr Manufacturing Company of Halifax began to produce skates for hockey players around the same time they developed their significant reputation among speed skaters. The Starr company began with skates with a wood platform, like the pair in my collection made in 1864, called "Starr Demon" and used by hockey players in Halifax. Under the toe of the wood platform is a long slot for the leather straps to secure the skate to the foot. There are also two screws at the toe and one at the heel that connect the leather to the wood plate.

As skate manufacturers shifted toward making their own boots, however, Starr's hockey skates changed to meet this new trend. Starr's "Ladies Beaver" skate, from 1888, was used for both hockey and recreation at the end of the century. While the name of this model targeted women, it was a model that all skaters liked, so Starr continued to offer it, with few changes, for many years.

BLADE LENGTH

Starr was not the only manufacturer that catered to both speed skating and hockey. J.A. Whelpley of New Brunswick, who was later hired by the Keene Manufacturing Company, was well known for his "Long Reach" skates, which he first made in 1859 (see "Blades with Holes" sidebar in the previous chapter). However, while the "Long Reach" skates were popular with locals in New Brunswick for transportation and communication—to get around the area's many rivers in winter—Keene seemed more interested in the skates for the sports market. While Keene

TOP Hockey skate
by J.A. Whelpley,
Greenwich, New
Brunswick, 1895.
COLLECTION OF JEAN-
MARIE LEDUC

BOTTOM Hockey
skate, Union
Hardware, Torrington,
Connecticut, ca 1870s.
COLLECTION OF JEAN-
MARIE LEDUC

continued to specialize in long blades, the company also dabbled in hockey skates. One of Whelpley's hockey skates, made in Greenwich, New Brunswick, in 1895, has a short blade, which is necessary for hockey. The blade shows some rust, a sign of how the skates were used and, perhaps, a sign of poor maintenance. Skates need to be properly dried after use to avoid rusting. Even the best pair of steel skates can rust without proper care. Not many Whelpley skates remain, so this pair is particularly valuable. Many years ago, Thom Overend, the chief technician for Speed Skating Canada, asked me if I had a pair of Whelpley skates in my collection. When I told him I did, he said, "You're very lucky."

Other companies vied for a share of the hockey market, but they had to somehow stand out from the rest to gain any traction. Union Hardware, in Torrington, Connecticut, produced a rare pair of American-made hockey skates. Since Union had such a sterling reputation, they ventured into hockey skates on a few occasions, although the market for hockey skates in the United States was small, so most American manufacturers focused on figure skates and long blades. One of Union's earliest forays into hockey skates dates to 1870. Clamping to footwear at both the heel and toe, this skate was then secured by using a thumbscrew under the heel. Made from hardened steel, this model shows how Union, despite being known for long blades, hoped to capitalize on an expanding hockey market.

Union tried to meet the needs of players, just like other skate manufacturers did. For a cast steel pair from 1905, Union responded to the complaint about pucks sliding through the space between the blade and the footplate: the design features a spike above the centre of the blade. So when these skates were screwed to a defenceman's boots, he could feel confident that he would not lose track of a puck that snuck through his skates. Compare that to a pair from six years earlier. Union clearly wanted to keep their customers happy by listening to their suggestions.

Skates were increasingly sold with boots attached, and Union continued to come up with new designs for the hockey market. At the same time, though, Union wanted to ensure its skates could be purchased by a lot of people, not just hockey players. They made a skate in the 1890s whose blade extends beyond both the toe and the heel, making it much longer than that of most hockey skates. Some players felt this gave them an edge by letting them go faster—some even used them for racing—without compromising their agility on the ice.

TOP Cast steel
hockey skate by
Union Hardware,
ca 1905. COLLECTION
OF JEAN-MARIE LEDUC

MIDDLE Hockey skate
by Union Hardware
Torrington, CT,
1890S. COLLECTION
OF JEAN-MARIE LEDUC

BOTTOM Cast steel
hockey skate by Union
Hardware, patented in
1899. COLLECTION OF
JEAN-MARIE LEDUC

"Joe" Lépine

ONE OF MY favourite pairs of skates combines blades with skis, attached to boots from another pair of skates. They were made around 1945 by a baseball player who would go on to play defence for the Montreal Canadiens, and who would stay with the organization for over forty years: Maurice "Joe" Lépine. He was from the Lowertown neighbourhood of Ottawa and liked to skate on the Rideau River in the winter. The frozen river was rarely cleared of snow. Eventually, he decided to make these skates, which feature a normal hockey blade of tempered steel surrounded by a ski. When he travelled over clean ice, he could skate normally, but when he hit a patch of snow, he could easily switch to skiing. The blade protrudes from the bottom of the ski, which, given the conditions, would have little effect on his skiing motion.

I like this pair not only because of their uniqueness, but also because of my personal connection to their maker. Joe was a member of l'Institut canadien-français d'Ottawa, an organization founded in 1852, for which I once served as cultural director and am currently a councillor. He was a well-liked man—following his death we had a big ceremony at l'Institut, attended by two of his former teammates.

ABOVE Handmade skate by Maurice "Joe" Lépine, Ottawa, ca 1945. COLLECTION OF JEAN-MARIE LEDUC

EXPERIMENTS WITH METAL

Once companies began producing their own boots to go with their blades, hockey skates in the nineteenth century took on a very standardized look, although certain aspects continued to be refined. Hockey players said their skates were too heavy and were slowing them down, so manufacturers looked for ways to reduce their weight any way they could. By the late nineteenth century, steel blades were standard, but they contributed a good portion of the weight. Perhaps a lighter metal could be used for the blade or elsewhere on a skate. The Canadian Cycle and Motor Company— better known as CCM—therefore began experimenting with aluminum. While blades could not be composed entirely of aluminum, because the metal is too weak, aluminum could replace the steel used elsewhere on the skate, like on a pair from 1905. The blades of the CCM "Automobile" skates are made with chrome nickel and laminated with steel, while the footplate is aluminum. The same model was also designed with the boots included. The hope was that by replacing the steel in the footplate with aluminum, the skates would be lighter but still as strong. That hope was soon dashed, however; the skates broke more frequently than the ones with steel footplates. As they were only produced for about twenty years, skates with an aluminum footplate are quite easy to date.

Despite the weakness that came with the aluminum footplate, "Automobile" skates were arguably the most popular model of hockey skates at the end of the nineteenth century. One of the main reasons was that CCM focused on making them comfortable. In one model of 1905 that came with a boot, for instance, a strap goes over the laces to help keep the skates tight on the foot. The tri-metal blade—chrome, nickel, and steel—is laminated and tempered to ensure its strength, but the boots are the real appeal of this model. Another pair, made of the same materials, features

one critical difference: a high heel. Patented in 1905, this model came a little later than other models of "Automobile" skates, but they were immediately popular with some skaters because the higher heel puts more pressure on the skater's toes, which improves speed.

Even though the "Automobile" skates were their most well liked, CCM produced several other models around the turn of the century. Hockey players appreciated the "Cycle" skate, which was not sold with boots. One pair, made in 1897 from laminated, tempered steel, also has the spike in the middle of the blade to stop pucks. Around the edge are holes for screwing or riveting the footplate to a boot. Known internally at CCM as "Model 25," these skates were particularly popular with women. Too often, the history of hockey is written from the perspective of the men who played the game. But as "Model 25," and other models,

TOP, LEFT "Automobile" skates by CCM, Weston, ON. Patented in 1905. COLLECTION OF JEAN-MARIE LEDUC

BOTTOM, LEFT Hockey skate, CCM, Weston, ON, 1905. COLLECTION OF JEAN-MARIE LEDUC

TOP, RIGHT "Automobile" skate by CCM, 1906. COLLECTION OF JEAN-MARIE LEDUC

BOTTOM, RIGHT "Cycle" skate by CCM, 1897. COLLECTION OF JEAN-MARIE LEDUC

demonstrates, women have also been playing hockey for a long time. Hockey skates targeted to women have greatly improved in the twentieth century. Back when former Ottawa mayor Charlotte Whitton played hockey at Queen's University, where she graduated in 1917, the skates were not nearly as good as they are today. As women's hockey has garnered greater attention around the world, the skates have reached the point where, today, there is no difference in quality.

The story of how a company with "cycle" and "motor" in its name ended up making hockey skates is part of the story of skates in Canada. The company's history, as documented by John A. McKenty in *The CCM Story*, published in 1946, was commissioned for the company's fiftieth anniversary. It began under Walter Massey, as part of the Massey-Harris company in 1896 and became CCM in 1899. Skates bearing the CCM name and logo first emerged in the second half of the 1890s. The company began producing them because bicycles, their primary product, did not sell during the winter, and they already had the basic material: metal scraps left from the production of bicycles and even cars at the CCM plant in Toronto. CCM quickly became known as a quality producer of hockey skates.

THE TUBE IN HOCKEY

While CCM was growing in popularity, an idea that had been used in speed skates for over a decade—the tube—was being adapted to hockey skates. The man credited with bringing the tube to hockey is William Hamilton Dunne, whose company, W.H. Dunne, made roller, figure, and speed skates in the first years of the twentieth century. After hearing about the tube, Dunne set upon designing a new hockey skate. Just as designers had hoped for with aluminum skates, Dunne thought that if he could reduce the weight of a skate without compromising

TOP Tube hockey skate designed by William Hamilton Dunne, Toronto, ON, 1905. COLLECTION OF JEAN-MARIE LEDUC

MIDDLE Hockey skate, Daoust Manufacturing, Montreal, QC, ca 1940. COLLECTION OF JEAN-MARIE LEDUC

BOTTOM "Senior" skate, Daoust Manufacturing, Montreal, QC, ca 1960. COLLECTION OF JEAN-MARIE LEDUC

its strength, hockey players would want his skates. His first tube skates were patented in 1905 and released a year later. The difference between these and older skates is quite apparent. Rather than attaching the blade to a full footplate, the blade is inserted into the tube, which connects to the boots in three places. These were lighter than all-steel skates, without compromising strength, so hockey players took an immediate interest in them—and not just because of the tube. The boots were solid and sturdy, offering good support. So while the tube was the major change, Dunne had a knack for producing high-quality skates overall—so much so that many players opted to use his skates rather than the CCM "Automobile" skates.

In fact, the skates were so popular that when the NHL was founded in 1917, Dunne's tube skate, as it was called, was the league's official skate. I have heard several versions from former players of how this came about. The most common one is this. Sidney Ballard, the father of Harold Ballard, who had been part of the Toronto Maple Leafs organization since 1940, including eighteen years as the team's owner, decreed that any player who did not wear tube skates would not be allowed to play in the league. While the connection between Ballard senior and the NHL is not clear, the Ballard family produced skates in the early twentieth century until the Depression. Harold Ballard was not well liked, and it is possible that when people found out his father was in the skate business, this legend slowly evolved. Whether the story is true or not, the vast majority, if not all, of NHL players used a version of the W.H. Dunne tube skate for most of the twentieth century.

People often ask about the changes to skates over the years, wanting to know what made the biggest difference to the various ice sports. When it comes to hockey, there is not a doubt in my mind that it was the tube skate. It fundamentally changed the way the sport is played. The skates allowed the players to go faster than ever before but were strong enough that they would not break under the extreme pressure. To see how effective the tube was, look at its longevity: for the better part of a century, it was the industry standard in hockey. NHL players would not think of playing with anything else. And as the skates got better, the sport improved and grew in popularity.

Skate manufacturers, however, have continued to look for other ways to improve hockey skates. Some of these manufacturers are well known and still produce skates today, but others were not able to sustain their success. A good example is Daoust, a Montreal company that had been making skates since the late nineteenth century. Officially called Daoust, Lalonde & Co, it produced boots and shoes and also became involved in skates. Like other manufacturers, Daoust incorporated the tube into their skates. In the pair from my collection from the 1940s, damage to the boot is evidence that the skates saw a lot of ice time, but, true to their reputation, these Daoust skates have withstood the wear and tear. A newer—and less beat up—pair from the 1960s feature a design in which a curved bar connects the heel to the back of the blade—a new safety feature. Apart from this, the two pairs are aesthetically very similar, with the most prominent difference being the colour used along the tongue under the laces.

Daoust made very good skates, but being in Montreal certainly helped their sales. Not only were the Montreal Canadiens the world's largest sports organization in the 1950s, as the *New York Times Magazine* wrote, but the area probably had the largest market for hockey in the world. In addition, Quebec's political environment changed in the post–Second World War years, with the Quiet Revolution and emergence of the sovereigntist movement in Quebec. A French-Canadian company that produced high-quality hockey skates was sure to be successful. It has now gone out of business—one of its main downfalls was a lack of advertising and brand recognition—but its skates continue to have a good reputation among hockey players and skate collectors. Fortunately, the company kept detailed records that we can now use to help identify its skates and get a sense of its decision-making process, which is particularly valuable when we examine their various models.

SAFETY FEATURES

Even with companies like Daoust making high-quality hockey skates, the design of skates did not radically change. Instead, such companies were continually making minor adjustments. The most notable of these improvements came in the area of protection. The earliest hockey skates with attached boots left the ankles vulnerable to injury—from pucks, sprains, and strains. In some cases, the leather was so thin that it would not stand up on its own. To display some pairs in my collection adequately, I have to insert a stick inside the boot to ensure the ankles do not flop over. Over time, boots became thicker. Some had plastic shells, others had layers of protective material in between leather layers, and the occasional pair even featured rubber ankle protection.

The added padding is not only important to save players' feet from speeding pucks, but also to provide greater support to the ankle structure as a whole, and the Achilles tendon in particular. That need was highlighted during the 1957–58 NHL season when Maurice "Rocket" Richard played only twenty-eight games before a torn Achilles tendon took him off the ice. Fortunately for his team's fans, he was able to return for the playoffs and led the Canadiens to their third consecutive Stanley Cup. The added weight resulting from increasing support and protection is always a concern, though. With new materials, manufacturers have been able to increase protection while actually reducing skates' weight. A boot on a skate made today can be as thin as some older pairs, but the new materials, like Kevlar, nylon, rubber, plexiglass, and foam, make them much safer.

Improvements in saftey emerged even while other hazards persisted. Even though the tube revolutionized hockey, for many years the back of the blade on tube skates came to a point. This was dangerous—it could get caught in another skate or piece of equipment or, even scarier, do some serious damage to another player. Hockey equipment hasn't always been as comprehensive as it is today. Players did not wear helmets or neck guards, for example, and it was much easier for a player to be cut by that point of the blade. One incident occurred on March 22, 1989, the night when an errant skate cut Buffalo Sabres goalie Clint Malarchuk in the neck. Fortunately, the team's trainer was a Vietnam War veteran and calmly got Malarchuk to the trainer's room and then the hospital without losing too much blood. Malarchuk has written a book in which he bluntly states that he should have died that night. Incidents like that are a reminder of how much damage a skate blade can do and why even a minor safety improvement can do a lot to help protect players.

A minor addition with a major effect was the plastic protector on the end of the blade, which can be seen on Bobby Hull's skates on page 121. And on the Daoust skate of the 1960s, which I described earlier, a curved bar connects the back of the blade to the heel of the boot. Because the tube was so popular, there was no way around the pointed blade, so the protective cover became an industry standard in the second half of the twentieth century—in fact it was approved by the NHL as a safety measure.

Bobby Hull

THE "SILVER ARROW" skates that I acquired in 1992 were made in Canada and are noteworthy because of what appears on the side of the boot: Bobby Hull's signature. The two-time Hart Trophy winner who won a Stanley Cup with the Chicago Blackhawks is regarded as one of the greatest players ever. I met Bobby Hull when I gave a talk to retired players. After the talk, we chatted for a bit, as he was quite interested in the history of skates and my collection. In addition to donating this pair, he thought the collection could be the basis for a book, because, he said, it was important for Canadians to learn more about the equipment that is so central to our national sport.

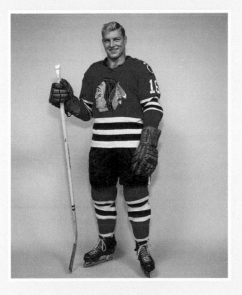

LEFT Bobby Hull in 1960 as a member of the Chicago Blackhawks. WEEKEND MAGAZINE/LOUIS JAQUES/LAC

RIGHT "Silver Arrow" CCM skates, autographed by Bobby Hull. COLLECTION OF JEAN-MARIE LEDUC

THE RISE OF BRAND NAMES

Smaller companies had difficulty in trying to find a market for their skates because consumers were so familiar with major brands, the biggest of which was, and continues to be, Bauer. Founded in 1927 in Kitchener, Ontario, Bauer promotes itself as the first company to sell skates with the blades attached to the boot. Early on, the company worked with Starr Manufacturing by providing the boots for Starr's blades. Starr actually called one pair from 1931 their "Bauer" skates. Despite the partnership, Bauer quickly earned its own reputation, based primarily on their "Supreme" skates. This model was by far Bauer's most popular and remains a staple of their product line today. The early "Supremes," as was the case for all Bauer hockey skates, used the tube in their designs.

Even though the "Supremes" were the most popular skates, Bauer experimented with other designs. One pair from the 1950s represents Bauer's efforts to attract female players to their brand. Named the "Special Bauer Beauty," this model incorporates a tube and has the look of a figure skate, but it is really a hockey skate. Two major clues tell us this: tubes were not used in figure

TOP "Special Bauer Beauty," women's hockey skate, Bauer, ca 1955. COLLECTION OF JEAN-MARIE LEDUC

MIDDLE "Juvenile" recreation skate, Bauer, late 1970s. COLLECTION OF JEAN-MARIE LEDUC

BOTTOM Pleasure skate, Bauer, ca 1960s. COLLECTION OF JEAN-MARIE LEDUC

skates and there are no stop picks at the toe. Compare those to a pair from the 1970s. These also look like figure skates, but in fact are neither figure nor hockey skates: they have neither tubes nor stop picks. So with this model, Bauer was hoping to attract skaters who liked to hit the ice for some fun and exercise, but not for sport. These were actually an updated version of another model from the 1960s, also used for recreational skating.

Bauer was able to produce skates like these because of the facilities they built around the country. The company invited me to speak to the Ontario Shoemakers Association about the history of skates at Bauer's Cambridge facility. They then gave me a tour of the facilities, where sometimes entire skates are custom-made. I watched a pair being made for a defenceman who wanted shock-absorbent skates. He never wore socks when he played, not an uncommon practice, because skaters think they get a better feel for the ice that way. Bauer used at least seven different materials for the boot, making it almost twice as thick as a normal one.

THE TUUK

Bauer is best known for its skates, though it produces a great deal of other related equipment. In fact, the company introduced the biggest change in hockey skates since the tube: the "Tuuk." Anyone who has played hockey or watched a game on television in the last thirty years will have noticed that none of the skates mentioned so far resemble a modern hockey skate. That is because the Tuuk—an innovation in plastic of the chassis, the piece that connects the blade to the boot—was not introduced until the late 1970s. In fact, when it was first used in the NHL, the cameramen were more interested in the players' feet than the play on the ice. Just like the tube, what was revolutionary about the Tuuk was that it significantly reduced the skate's weight, so players immediately wanted it on their boots.

LEFT "Hugger" hockey skate, Bauer, patented in 1976. COLLECTION OF JEAN-MARIE LEDUC

In one of the first pairs of Bauer skates with the Tuuk, the difference from the tube skate is quite striking. The Tuuk is connected to the boot at the heel and toe with rivets—it is like a footplate, as the top spans the entire foot, but it gets thinner closer to the blade. The opening in the middle keeps it light while also providing a gap for snow, which helps with stopping. The Tuuk is hollow and the blade is attached with small bolts that are connected from the inside. It is also moulded using Zytel plastic, which is extremely strong and can withstand the pressure of skating and the impact of a 100-mile-per-hour slap shot without shattering. The Bauer "Hugger" skate was patented in Canada in 1976, a year before the Tuuk made its NHL debut.

In the collection are several Tuuk chassis, without the boot, that demonstrate some experimentation with the form. One is a "Stainless Titanium" model from 1976, showing the basic form of the Tuuk. The centre above the blade is hollowed out, and the rivet holes that connect the skate to the boot are visible. For the most part, the Tuuk has stayed the same, but there are some exceptions. In another model, the "Super Steel," the centre gap is further back in the foot to accommodate a hole at the toe, an innovation intended to reduce the skate's weight, but it did not

catch on because the wider gap reduced its strength. The blade of the "Tuuk Plus" model, from 1980, is thinner at the toe than it is at the heel, a feature intended to give the blade better bite in the ice by forcing the foot's pressure forward. However, sharpening machines only work when the blade's thickness is uniform, so this model was removed from the market soon after its release.

Another benefit of the Tuuk was that it eliminated the point of the blade at the heel. The blade rounds off at the back and now has a small plastic guard that extends beyond the metal to further protect against accidents.

OTHER INNOVATIONS

In the forty years since Bauer introduced the Tuuk, hockey skates have undergone a few more changes, though none as significant as the Tuuk. Companies have experimented with boot design by using new materials to improve their strength and stability while simultaneously reducing weight. Recently they have also experimented with heated blades. These can be charged between periods and, the theory goes, can improve speed by making it easier for the skates to create water under the blade.

Another new development has been the introduction of a blade coated with many layers of carbon. This blade is designed to improve speed. Mounted in a Tuuk by Bauer, it is made from stainless steel and covered with four coats of carbon. Without increasing the blade's weight, this carbon blade is more effective than other blades in creating the film of water that allows a skater to move forward on the ice, which helps players conserve energy over the course of a game. Sold under the name "BlackEdge," the skates have only been available for the past ten years, but they are already being worn by some members of the Boston Bruins.

In 2011, Bauer tested the innovative "trigger blade," a removable blade; the company produced 10,000 pairs the next year. A trigger blade is inserted in a Tuuk chassis and locked. When the blade needs to be changed, the skater simply pulls the trigger under the heel, removes the blade, and inserts the new blade, which clicks into place. Changing a blade is much faster and easier than changing skates. Before this, to replace a blade, you would have to first remove the Tuuk from the boot by taking out the connecting screws. Getting a new pair was much more efficient. Now, if a blade is damaged during a play, it can be replaced almost immediately. A second generation of trigger blade skates is currently in production.

The sport of sledge hockey has also evolved because of innovative ways of thinking about skate blades. The blades on the sledges are the same as those on a pair of hockey skates, except that a sledge has two blades. Because they are sharpened in the same way as a hockey skate, with the same edges and rocker, the player has same the ability to abruptly change directions, stop on a dime, and accelerate quickly. The sledges themselves may not

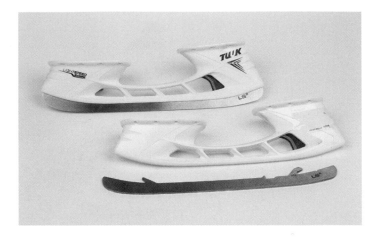

be considered skates, but it is the technology of skates that puts those athletes in a position to excel.

Despite these latest improvements, I am skeptical that another major change to hockey skates will emerge—at least in the short term. Manufacturers can play with the weight and make small alterations to the design, but it is hard to imagine that something as revolutionary as the tube or the Tuuk will appear anytime soon. The tube was the standard for three-quarters of a century before the Tuuk took its place forty years ago. From the skates clamped to boots that players used in the late 1800s, hockey skates have come a long way, and as a result, so has the game of hockey. And because of that, the game itself has improved.

The
Final Lap

I AM ALWAYS VERY moved when I see how skates can bring people together. When my wife and I head over to the Rideau Canal on a clear day in February, people are having a good time on the ice—from children who can barely walk to octogenarians, some of whom can also barely walk. The youngest I have seen skating was a three-and-a-half-year-old, while the oldest I've seen in a competition was a ninety-two-year-old from Los Angeles. Skating is a lifelong activity. While hunters travelling along the St. Lawrence in the seventeenth century had a different reason for skating than a young couple enjoying the frozen waterway on a Saturday afternoon in 1901 or 2017, their activities and their skates show how integral skating is to Canada and how, despite the technological changes in skates, there is an aspect of skating that is truly timeless.

There is also something about skating that brings out the best in people. During the Special Olympics Winter Games in 1997, I had the pleasure of announcing the speed skating competition. Members of the Belarusian delegation came to watch some of the early races and expressed their interest in speed skating. Four of five of them were registered to compete in hockey, but they had never seen or participated in speed skating relays. We appointed each one a coach for the relay race competition. They could not speak English nor could we find a coach who spoke either Belarusian or Russian, so the organizing committee brought in translators, an addition of people that made things even more complicated. But they were determined. They practised one hour each morning, followed by another hour at night, and they were always there, working as hard as they could to learn relay racing.

They borrowed speed skates, but we were so short of skates that
they had to take turns using them, which certainly slowed down
the learning. After three days, they began to get comfortable on
the skates that require such a different technique from hockey.
They also seemed to understand the basic rules of relays, but they
still had a long way to go before they could compete.

One of the obstacles was a general lack of equipment. They
had not come to Canada to participate in relay racing, so they
lacked not just speed skates but also helmets, gloves, and body
suits. And they did not have the funding to buy this equipment.
So one of our Ontario representatives called Canadian Tire to
explain what was going on, and two days later a truck arrived at
the arena with all the equipment the Belarusians needed.

It was an amazing gift and really lifted their spirits—they had
been working so hard, and now they had the chance to skate in

one of the relay races. While that made a lot of sense, there was some skepticism: a lot of people are on the ice during a relay, and if you do not have a strong grasp of the rules, it can get confusing out there. But they were steadfast. And a week after seeing the sport for the first time and wanting to give it a shot, they were on the podium with bronze medals around their necks. Everyone was so happy for them. Of all the races I had the chance to announce, that one stands out as one of my favourites.

Those are the types of stories that, to me, are emblematic of skating. At its core, this is a country of good people who look out for each other, something I always think about when I look at my skate collection and think about how those skates came to be there. The people I've met through speed skating and through my collection have showed me that community spirit and goodwill are alive and well.

I think that helps to account for why people have such strong reactions when they come to my exhibitions. This is particularly true of older visitors, for whom the skates bring back cherished memories—those tears in their eyes tell me that they see more than boots with metal blades; they see the times and places of their lives that now elicit powerful emotions.

Each pair of skates in this book represents some part of our history, and so they are valuable artifacts. A great variety of skates are specialized, unique, innovative, or even failures that do not mark a major step in the evolution of skating. They are the product of efforts to address problems—both with older designs and the conditions in which people were using them. Progress is not possible without failure. There have to be challenges along the way. The tube and the clap skate propelled skates and ice sports forward, but other ideas were just as important in the process. Those skates from athletes like Butch Bouchard, Gaétan Boucher, and Barbara Ann Scott—and the things those

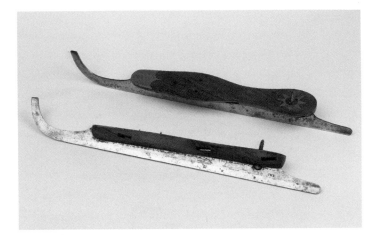

remarkable athletes were able to do—are a testament to the work that went into developing new concepts. Not all new concepts work, but they are all part of that journey. People respond to local conditions, think of ways to expand their market, and try new ways to improve performance. Even though some of those ideas have not been incorporated into modern skates, they made major contributions.

My hope is that Canadians share my passion to explore this vital history and that the stories, both positive and negative, of this country's experiences on ice will be preserved for future generations. After all, each winter, millions of Canadians head to the rink to lace up.

Further Reading

Copley-Graves, Lynn. *Figure Skating History: The Evolution of Dance on Ice*. Columbus, OH: Platoro Press, 1992.

Formenti, Federico, and Alberto E. Minetti. "Human Locomotion on Ice: The Evolution of Ice-Skating Energetics through History." *Journal of Experimental Biology*. 210(10) (2007): 1825–1833.

Herner, Russell. *Antique Ice Skates for the Collector*. Atglen: Schiffer Publishing, 2000.

Hines, James R. *Figure Skating: A History*. Urbana/Colorado Springs: University of Illinois Press/World Figure Skating Museum and Hall of Fame, 2006.

Luik, Heidi, et al., eds. *From Hooves to Horns, from Mollusc to Mammoth: Manufacture and Use of Bone Artefacts from Prehistoric Times to the Present*. Proceedings of the 4th Meeting of the ICAZ Worked Bone Research Group at Tallinn, 26th–31st of August 2003. Muinasaja teadus 15. Talinn, Estonia: 2005.

Marks, Don. *They Call Me Chief: Warriors on Ice*. Winnipeg, MB: J.G. Shillingford, 2008.

McKenty, John A. *Canada Cycle & Motor: The CCM Story—1899–1983*. Belleville: Epic Press, 2011.

McKinley, Michael. *Hockey: A People's History.* Toronto: McClelland and Stewart, 2009.

Petkevich, John Misha. *The Skater's Handbook.* New York: Charles Scribner's Sons, 1984.

Publow, Barry. *Speed on Skates.* Champlain, IL: Human Kinetics, 1999.

"Sonja Henie," obituary, *New York Times*, October 13, 1969.